KEN WATSON
ON CURLING

KEN WATSON

CANADIAN CHAMPIONSHIP FINALS, 1949

Ken Watson On Curling

by
Ken
Watson

Foreword by Gordon M. Hudson

THE COPP CLARK PUBLISHING COMPANY

VANCOUVER   TORONTO   MONTREAL

[1700]

Foreword

By GORDON M. HUDSON, President, Dominion Curling Association, 1949-50, and Winner of Dominion Curling Championships in 1928 and 1929.

In my opinion, there is no one in Canada better qualified to write a book on curling for beginners and experts than Ken Watson.

Ken Watson not only possesses great curling ability, but his scholarly attainments qualify him to teach others. He can practise what he preaches and also preach what he practises. His success has been so great, and his record is so impressive, that he is sometimes referred to in the press as "Mr. Curler". He is a leading exponent of scientific curling. His success has been achieved by strategy as well as great mechanical ability.

Curling is no longer regarded as an old man's game, and the younger generation is filling the curling rinks to capacity. The time is ripe for a sound and complete text book. A close reading of this book will not only enable the reader to play a better game, but, through appreciating the finer points, he will get a great deal more pleasure and enjoyment out of the play.

I have been active in the game for a great many years, and I have found the book interesting, enjoyable, and well worth while.

Contents

Glossary

BACK-BOARDS
—The boards or bumper behind each sheet of ice that mark the end of the sheet.

BACK-RING
—Usually refers to that portion of the eight-foot and twelve-foot rings behind the tee line.

BIG END
—To score four or more points in one end.

BITER
—A stone barely touching the outside ring.

CHAP AND LIE
—When a stone played strikes a corner of a stone and rolls to another position in the rings.

CHIP
—See "wick". A chip is usually finer or thinner than a wick.

CLOSE A PORT
—To block an opening between two stones.

COUNTER
—A stone in the rings closer to the centre than any opponent's stones.

CROSS HANDLE
—A handle of a stone when it points laterally across the ice or the body of the player.

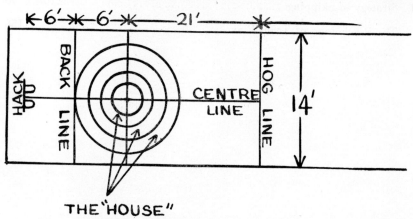

THE "HOUSE"
OR "HEAD"
OR "RINGS"
OR "CIRCLES"

CUP (OF A STONE) —A concave area approximately five inches wide on the under surface of a stone.

DRAW WEIGHT —Sufficient momentum to enable a stone delivered to reach the tee line.

END —An end is played when all players of both teams have delivered two stones each.

FREEZE —A term used when one stone lies directly or almost directly in front of, and touching, another.

FRONT RINGS —Usually refers to that portion of the eight-foot and twelve-foot rings in front of the tee line.

GOOSE NECK —The curve of the handle of the stone that connects the handle with the bolt in the stone.

GUARD —Any stone in front of another.

HACK —The foot support or brace at each end of the ice sheet.

HEAD —Another term for the rings.

"THE HOUSE" —The rings or circles to which the stones are being played.

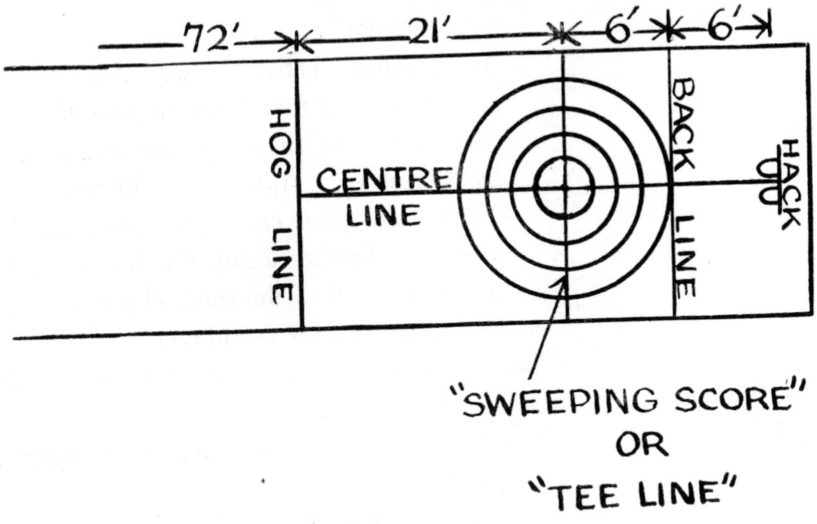

"SWEEPING SCORE"
OR
"TEE LINE"

IN-TURN	—A moving stone whose handle is turning in a clockwise manner.
LAST ROCK	—The last stone played during an end.
LEAD	—The first man on a curling team. He is called the lead because he delivers the first stone.
MATE	—Another term used to designate the third man.
NARROW	—A stone delivered inside the imaginary line to the skip's broom.
"ON THE BROOM"	—A stone delivered exactly on the imaginary line to the skip's broom.
OUT-TURN	—A moving stone whose handle is turning counter-clockwise.
OVER-DRAW WEIGHT (OVER TEE-WEIGHT)	—A stone with just sufficient motion to pass the tee line or back rings.
PEBBLE	—Formation produced on the surface of the ice by sprinkling of water.
PLAYDOWN	—A method used to determine a winner in curling competition involving many teams.
POCKET	—Stones in a semi-circular position concentric to the rings.
POINTS	—See "counter".
PORT	—An opening between two stones large enough for another stone to pass through.
PULL	—The amount of change in the course taken by a stone as it slides down the ice.
RAISE	—Term used when one stone moves another ahead or further along the line of direction to the end of the sheet of ice.
ROCK	—The stone used by the player.
ROLL	—Any movement of one stone after it strikes another.
RUB	—The grazing of one stone on another in passing.
RUNNER	—A very fast moving stone.

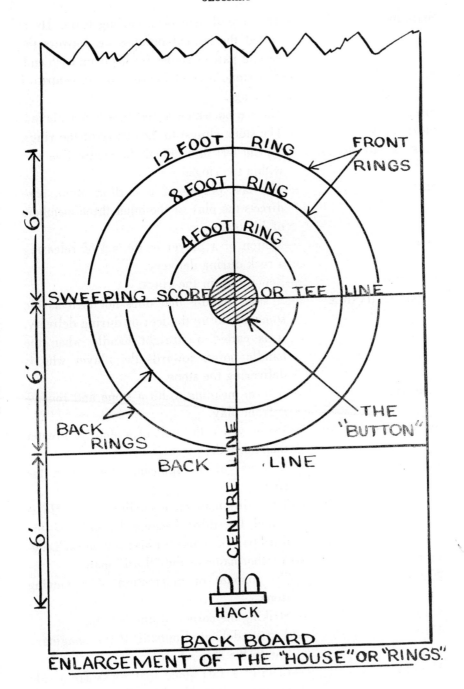

ENLARGEMENT OF THE "HOUSE" OR "RINGS."

SECOND

—The second man on a curling team. He is called the second because he delivers the second pair of stones for his team each end.

SECOND SHOT (STONE)

—The stone second nearest to the centre of the rings.

SHEET

—The ice on which a match is being played.

SHOT ROCK

—The stone closest to the centre of the rings.

SIDE OF THE HOUSE

—To the left or right of the centre line and within the rings.

SKIP

—The last player of a curling team, who directs the play of the other three members of his team.

SLIDE

—Motion of a player in the act of releasing a rock during delivery.

STICKING

—Remaining in the rings.

STRAIGHT HANDLE

—A stone handle that does not turn as the stone moves up the ice; or during delivery, it is called a straight handle when the handle points towards the player who is delivering the stone.

STRIKING

—A term meaning to hit a stone and remove it from play.

SWINGY ICE

—Ice on which the pull of a stone is greater than normal.

TAKE-OUT

—Removal of an opposing stone from the rings.

THIRD

—The third man on a curling team. He is called the third because he delivers the third pair of stones for his team on each end.

VICE-SKIP

—Another name of the "third" man.

WEIGHT

—The amount of momentum of a moving stone.

WICK

—Striking the corner of another stone.

WIDE

—A stone delivered outside of the imaginary line to the skip's broom.

WOBBLER

—Usually a fast stone that rocks from side to side as it moves down the ice.

Introduction

Participation in more than two thousand games of curling, over a span of thirty years, playing in club games, novelty bonspiels, district bonspiels, Provincial bonspiels, Mid-summer bonspiels, Canadian Championship playdowns, spoon competitions, mixed bonspiels, International matches, and running the gamut of natural ice, artificial ice, wet ice, frosty ice, alkali ice, up and downhill ice, machine-pebbled ice, and playing with sharp rocks, smooth rocks, light rocks, heavy rocks, in company with Premiers and tradesmen, university professors and high school boys, ministers and hotelkeepers, has left a multitude of impressions on my mind. From them a number of concepts have crystallized, which I shall endeavour to record in the following chapters of this book.

Any game worth playing is worth playing well. Curling is no exception. Yet there are tens of thousands of curlers whose only introduction to the game was a demonstration by a friend or a first skip illustrating the difference between an in-turn and an out-turn, with the possible added injunction to put which foot in what hack and keep the eye on the broom.

In spite of the inadequacies of proper coaching and teaching of the simple fundamentals of delivery, judgment of ice, and curling strategy, an amazing number of curling enthusiasts have achieved a measure of perfection after long years of trial and error, imitation, observation, and practice. But with the present popularity of the game attracting thousands of new devotees each year, both young and old, the problem of accommodation is becoming acute, and the task of finding time and space for coaching and teaching the new-comers is more remote than ever. To date very little effort has been devoted to reducing to writing the fundamental skills required by a good curler, and the methods by which they can be achieved.

The primary purpose of this book is to provide a simple yet comprehensive approach to these problems so that it may be used as a continual source of reference by both the beginner and the expert. It is to be hoped, too, that those interested in coaching and teaching the younger members, particularly those of school age who are being attracted to the game in large numbers, will find a simple basis of procedure for instruction. No attempt has been made to provide solutions for technical, financial, engineering problems that confront all curling clubs. This book is for the player, in an attempt to increase his proficiency and skill in making his shots, in understanding the strategy of the game, in helping him to grasp the importance of the psychology of team play, thereby increasing the enjoyment and satisfaction he will derive from being a member of one of the greatest fraternities in the world.

CHAPTER 1

Fundamentals of Delivery

No two curlers deliver a stone alike. Each has a peculiarity, however slight, that distinguishes him from others. It may be a preliminary waggle of his broom, a hunch of the shoulders, or particular
inclination of the head. Gordon Hudson, a famous two-time winner
of the Canadian Curling Championship, always rubs his gloved right
hand on his knee before beginning his backswing. Another famous
curler touches the peak of his cap before commencing. Others cup
the palm of the right hand and blow into it. In fact, after you have
observed certain players for years, it is not necessary to see the face
of a curler in the hack in order to name him. I know one very
observant member in my own club who, by asking spectators to
describe the details of action of certain skips delivering their stones
from the hack, can tell fairly accurately what the score of the game
is at the time.

In view of such variations in the delivery motion of individuals,
it might not seem very consistent to say that the delivery technique of
most top-notch curlers is fundamentally the same. Yet such is the
case. Slight deviations in positions of hands, arms, shoulders, or
legs do not alter the smoothness of the style, nor is the delivery of a
good player who delivers his rock without leaving the hack basically
different from an individual like myself who uses a long slide. Ask
Bob Gourlay, 1931 Dominion Championship Skip, or Howard Wood,
three times a member of Canadian Championship rinks, neither of
whom leave the hack in delivery, and both will tell you that whether
you slide or do not slide, that follow-through is essential to the smooth
delivery of the stone. I would ask the reader, then, when reading
this chapter or subsequent ones, to remind himself that in all descriptions, unless direct reference is made to the sliding delivery, all
statements refer simply to the basic essentials of any smooth, well-
co-ordinated delivery.

The importance of mastering the mechanics of a well-balanced swing or delivery in curling cannot be over-emphasized. Even after hours of practice and many years of play, you will often find it necessary to take a mental check on them even in the midst of an important match. During the 1949 Canadian Playdowns at Hamilton, we had played six ends against Northern Ontario. The score was almost even but we hadn't been playing too steadily. My brother Grant, at third rock, had been having trouble with his delivery. His swing was consistently wide of the broom, or you might say he was swinging his rock backward and forward along a line just outside of a straight line to the skip's broom at the other end of the ice. The result was a few misses in trying to hit Northern Ontario stones by being what curlers call "wide of the broom". As a skip, I always watch the arc of the swing of a stone thrown by any player on my team or on the opposing team, and I noticed that Grant's last two back-swings were outside the imaginary line to my broom. This meant simply that the position of his stone on the ice at the beginning of his backswing was not on a spot in line with my broom. When he came up the ice after delivering his stones on that end, I called him to the hack behind the rings and sat down in the hack with him to demonstrate. From then on he never missed a take-out of the opponents rocks when called for. Incidentally, we went on to win the game by a reasonably safe margin. Don't get the idea that there have not been occasions when I had to be given a dose of the same treatment by brother Grant.

In addition to the example given above, there are many reasons why a good delivery is important. Let me enumerate them.

1. *Perfect Balance*: Perfect balance in delivery gives you the "feel" of the stone which is indispensable in getting the correct weight. Often times I have had to check myself at the beginning or in the middle of a delivery, stop, and then start all over again, because I didn't feel perfectly balanced.

2. *A Groored Swing*: Any curler will philosophize occasionally in admonishing one who he thinks is greener to the intricacies of the game than he is, by saying: "Get the broom and the weight, and you'll get the shot." This over-worked statement covers a multitude

of tense situations, but it represents all ten commandments rolled into one as far as curling law is concerned. It is an adage that should be repeated by every curler before he plays every shot, in order to get him to the proper degree of concentration required.

There is only one sure way of "getting the broom" consistently that I am aware of, and that is through the process of developing by constant practice *a grooved swing,* similar to the goal of every ardent golfer. Actually there is only one way to develop a grooved swing and that is to construct a robot and place a curling stone in the mechanical hand. What all curlers strive for is something that is as close to a perfect grooved swing as possible. Perfection, thank God, is impossible. So, being human, with normal or abnormal muscular and nerve reflexes, we must cultivate a swing that is as natural, as effortless, and as rhythmic as possible. Once this has been mastered, the degree of perfection may reach 80% in a given game.

3. *Lack of Muscular Tension:* The more relaxed you are physically, the better chance you have of a rhythmic swing. This physical relaxation is all the more important because in competitive play nervous tension is great (or should be) and transmits itself with electrifying results to tense muscles. How often have you seen a player in the heat of an exciting game suddenly give the handle of the stone a violent twist as it leaves his hand?

4. *Getting the Broom:* Your skip holds his broom on the ice at the other end of the sheet you are playing on, as a target for you to aim at. Naturally, it is there for a purpose whether you believe he has put it in the right place or not. Let us assume that, for the weight you are going to play, his broom is in the right place. Then if your swing (both backswing and forward swing) is on a direct line with the broom you will make the shot. Then you will beam with satisfaction and your skip will give his opposing skip a sly look to see how much it has upset his equilibrium. But that is only one shot. There are thousands more to come. Can you make them all just as perfectly? That will depend on whether all future deliveries are on a smooth, unwavering line with your skip's broom at the other end. If your balance pulls your backswing off-line a fraction of an inch, if in

giving the handle of the stone its turn on the forward swing your line is affected, you will not get the result you hope for. If your backswing and forward swing are perfectly on the correct line, and your follow-through disturbs the line, similarly you are in for trouble.

What does a professional golfer concentrate on in his practice and in his teachings? The same principles you should be conscious of in curling: namely, the stance, the grip, the backswing, the forward swing, and the follow-through. All are separate parts of the swing, yet each is co-ordinated into a smooth-flowing effortless motion. The feet, hands, arms, legs, trunk, shoulders and head move in complete harmony with each other. And when perfect co-ordination is effected the golf pro hits them straight down the middle, and the curler "hits" the broom. We will not go into the matter of differences in weight here, our first concern is to get the swing. Let us step out onto the ice for a few minutes so that we can start with the first lesson.

THE DELIVERY

Preparing the Stone for Delivery

Many an important shot has been missed because of inadequate precautions taken in preparing the stone for delivery. How well I remember an all-important match in the semi-finals of the Manitoba Provincial Playdowns! We were playing the tenth end of a twelve-end match, with the score 8-7 against us. When my turn came to play my first stone we were lying four shot rocks. It only remained for me to play my two stones well to count a big end and, with last shot in my favour, such a score on the tenth end, which is crucial in any twelve-end game, would have given us a decided edge. At the second "hog" line my first stone picked up a loose straw, and instead of drawing nicely into the house for the fifth counter it ground to a stop six feet short of the twelve-foot circle. The opposing skip, Ness Wise of our own Club, played a very accurate take-out shot and rolled perfectly in behind my stone. With my last shot I failed in an attempt to negotiate the guard and pass his stone through for the four points. Sad to relate, this was the turning point and we lost the game. Here is the point I am trying to get at. I do not blame the straw for the cause of our misfortune, rather I blame myself for carelessness in not cleaning my stone so carefully before delivery that the chance of its picking up such a straw would have been negligible.

Once a player gets into the hack his first responsibility is to clean the "cup" or running surface of his stone thoroughly so that not one speck of grit, dirt, or straw adheres to it. Even a small particle of foreign matter on the rim of the "cup" will act as a gatherer of other substances as it travels down the ice, because it elevates the rim enough to allow straws and dirt to get under the stone and affect its momentum. A well-polished cup on normally clean ice will push any straw aside that lies in its path. This is particularly true after the pebble has worn off. Draw shots are

Fig. 1

CLEANING THE STONE

Here the right hand is used to give the stone two or three turns on the broom straw to clean the cup. After this operation, the rock should be turned over and examined, to ensure that all dirt has been removed.

more seriously affected than running shots, so in playing the former be as fussy as a Dutch housewife in ascertaining that the running surface of your stone, as well as the ice surface immediately in front of the hack, is spotlessly clean. Too often I have seen a curler assiduously clean off his stone then turn it over right side up and set it carefully down right in the midst of the corruption that he had just brushed off his stone.

How to Clean the Cup of the Stone

There are two methods commonly used to clean the cup, both of which leave little to chance. The first is to place your broom flat on the ice holding it with the left hand, then with the right hand lift your stone on to the long straw of your broom and twirl the stone several times (see Fig. 1). Lift the stone off the straw carefully, then flip it over to make certain that every last vestige of dirt has been removed. Finally, before righting the stone, use your broom to clean the ice surface immediately in front of the hack so that when your stone is placed on the ice ready for delivery the surfaces of both the stone and the ice are perfectly clean. All this preparation can be done from a sitting position in the hack.

Fig. 2

CLEANING THE STONE

The player has turned over the rock and is using the long straw of his broom to remove all dirt from the cup or running surface of the stone. Notice that the stone is well to the left of centre line so that any dirt will be brushed to one side and away from the line of delivery. This method of cleaning the stone is the most commonly accepted practice.

The second method is one I favour myself as leaving least to chance. Flip the stone over with a quick forward then backward jerk of the right hand. Then with the up-turned rock lying on its handle and gripped between the knees, take the long straw of the broom with both hands and give the cup a thorough scrubbing (see Fig. 2). Before righting the stone, use the broom again with your right hand to sweep aside all dirt immediately in front of the hack. Once the stone has been turned over, a final precaution is taken. While sitting in the hack, preparing for delivery, the stone is pulled slowly back and forth once or twice with the fingers holding the handle lightly, to assure the player that there is still nothing on the rim of the cup to make the stone stick. Many, many times, before an important draw shot, I have flipped the stone over again for a last reassuring look at the running surface.

Fig. 3

THE STANCE (from right)

The right arm is extended without tension. The hand and fingers are relaxed. The line along the right thigh from the hip to the knee points directly at the stone. The body is inclined forward slightly and the right toe in the hack is in line with the right arm. The position is one of comfort and ease.

Fig. 4

STANCE (from left)

This photograph allows a glimpse of the relative positions of the left leg, left arm and left foot during the stance. Note the left foot flat on the ice and well under the knee. The left thigh is parallel to the ice and the left arm is extended in almost a direct lateral position to the body.

The Stance (Position in the hack—see Figs. 3 and 4)

As in golf, baseball, and all sports where a player is getting set to deliver or swing, the position of the relative parts of the body in relation to the swing is of major importance if complete co-ordination is to be effected. The important thing to remember about the stance is that you should be in a position where you are comfortable and thereby completely relaxed. As the prime object of developing a good delivery is to help get the broom and the weight consistently, any curler will readily admit that the easier and the more natural his efforts are, the less chance of error. My chief concern in describing for you the mechanics of a good delivery, which to my mind is the most important of all fundamentals in curling, is not to encourage the experienced player to try any radical changes in his time-tried style nor to suggest to the beginner that he attempt to carry this book along in his hip pocket for reference every time he gets into the hack, but rather, through the illustrations and observations offered in the following pages, to help some of you to gain through constant practice and play, the "feel" of natural and unhesitating rhythm of movement in the delivery of your stone. Once you get that "feel" which comes from perfect balance, a free, natural swing, and a relaxed follow-through, curling will give you so much more enjoyment, pride of achievement, and satisfaction.

Position of the Feet (Assuming the player is right-handed)

The key to balance in the hack is *the right foot*. It is the pivot which carries the full weight of the body and the rock during the swing. The ball of the right foot should rest squarely on the back of the hack with the toe of the shoe pointing as nearly straight ahead as possible (see Fig. 5). The position of the right foot in the hack determines the position of the body, which should at all times be squarely facing up the ice in the direction the stone is to be thrown. If the right toe is placed sideways in the hack, the body has a tendency to turn in the same direction, and if you try to pull the shoulders and trunk and hips around so that they are at right angles to the delivery line, the muscles of the right leg must be tensed in order to take this unnatural position. Such tension is injurious to a free and easy swing, so avoid it by placing the foot in the hack in a natural standing position.

This brings up the problem of hacks. The dimensions of a hack are supposed to be standard and if they are, they will accommodate the correct position of the right foot easily. The safest and surest footing is provided by the new standard rubber hack. The back-board of many hacks often becomes covered with ice and this makes footing insecure. The ice coat must be scraped off before it is safe to use such a hack. Another common fault is a shallow hack which, if icy, catches the toe of the right foot at the beginning of the swing and causes it to slip, with consequent disaster to the delivery. The ideal

Fig. 5 — POSITION OF THE FEET IN THE HACK

The ball of the foot is placed squarely on the back of the hack, with the line of direction of the right shoe parallel to the sides of the hack and the centre line. The position of the left foot can be seen also. It is slightly ahead of the right foot and is placed flat on the ice in its natural positions with the toe inclined slightly to the left. The relaxed "sitting on the right heel" stance position is apparent here and is recommended as the most natural stance position.

hack is one that has a non-skid back-board, is deep enough to allow the toe of the right foot to dip into it without slipping, and tapered sufficiently toward the front end so as not to catch the toe if it leaves the hack on the follow-through. The diagrams below will illustrate what the right foot does in the hack during the delivery of the stone.

The position of the left foot is determined by the type of stance used by the player, or the style of crouch he is accustomed to. The prime object is to gain comfort and the feeling of sure-footed balance.

Lawn Bowling and quoits require a delivery, or swing, very much similar to that in curling, but because the game of curling is played on a slippery, ice surface and the object to be delivered is much heavier (a curling stone averages 42 lbs.) than those used in the other pastimes, curlers have adopted many weird postures in trying to get a safe delivery stance. The chief variations in the position of

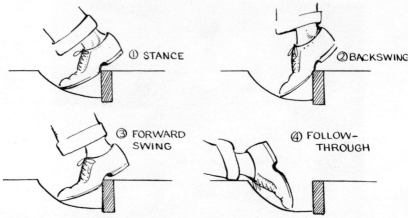

the left foot are determined by the uprightness of the stance before delivery. The more elevated the body, the farther forward the left foot is placed. Personally, I favour a very compact position, which might be called a sitting stance, the left foot just slightly ahead of the right foot. This is accomplished by sitting back on the right heel (see Fig. 3). The more compact the stance, the less chance of error in the line of the backswing, and consequently the more consistent the shot-making.

Position of the Knees and Thighs

Irrespective of the style of crouch or stance used, both knees and thighs should be as nearly parallel with the delivery line as is possible for natural ease and comfort (see Fig. 6). Either knee or thigh pointing too much off line tends to turn the hips and shoulders away from the correct right-angle position (see Fig. 7). Under no circumstances should the right knee rest on the ice. If the knee is kept elevated and parallel to the ice, it is easy to keep the trunk, head, and shoulders in a fairly upright position, irrespective of whether a long or a compact stance is used.

Position of the Arms, Shoulders and Head

If you examine Fig. 3 carefully, you will notice *the right arm* extended its full length yet without rigidity or tension. The stone is just far enough forward to cause the full extension of this arm without affecting in any way the position of the shoulders, hips,

Fig. 6

THE STANCE (front view)

Note the relaxed sitting position in the hack. The stone and handle are set for an in-turn delivery. Both thighs are parallel to centre line. The hips, shoulders, and chest are at right angles to the line of delivery. The right shoulder has dropped a little. The right arm reaches forward easily toward the stone. The feet are close together and in a compact position, while the head is erect and the eyes are focused on the broom at the other end of the sheet.

trunk, or head. It is vitally important that the right arm be kept straight during the entire swing but without any muscle tension. It is important, too, that the use of the right arm during the delivery should not alter the relative position of the hips, trunk, shoulders, and head. Too much reaching with the right hand during the stance will pull the right shoulder forward, forcing the left shoulder back; similarly, the hips and trunk will be pulled off line.

The left arm acts automatically as a counterbalance to the right arm, and because the weight of the stone during the backswing will tend to pull the body to the right side, the left arm extended to the side will help balance the body. Holding a broom with the left hand and arm extended is a "must" for a curler who wants a well-balanced delivery. The weight of a curling stone pulling on the right side of the body will force the right shoulder down and cause the hips and trunk of the body to turn off line to counteract this weight if the left hand and arm do not do their part in keeping the body in an erect position so that it faces the sheet of ice squarely at all times during the delivery motion. It matters little whether you grasp the broom at the top of the handle, as is shown in Fig. 7, or down shaft near the shoulder of the straw as long as in so doing you feel an easy,

Fig. 7—INCORRECT STANCE

Charlie Read exaggerates many common errors seen in the stance. Note the knees off line, shoulders and hips twisted, lack of compactness and balance, grasping of handle by fist instead of fingers, and awkward use of the broom to aid a balanced swing.

steady balance. A word of caution is in order as to the angle of extension of the left arm. My experience in coaching younger curlers has been that any tendency to extend the arm back and behind the body, pulls the shoulder off line and therefore creates an erratic forward swing and follow-through. This is particularly true with anyone attempting the sliding delivery. Personally, I favour the extension of the left arm to the side and about twenty degrees forward (see Fig. 3), and in any event no further back than a direct lateral extension.

You will no doubt have gathered from the foregoing paragraphs that *the shoulders* should at all times and during all phases of the delivery be kept parallel to the ice surface and at right angles to the delivery line. This means no dipping or twisting or any motion of

Fig. 8A

An Out-Turn Delivery

The only difference between an in-turn and an out-turn delivery is found in the position of the handle of the stone, and the movements of the right arm and hand. Compare with Fig. 15. During the backswing there is little or no change in the position of the handle.

Fig. 8B

At the top of the backswing.

Fig. 8C

The forward swing. The turn of the handle has commenced.

Fig. 8D

The release of an out-turn. The stone handle is pointing straight back. Note the position of the right hand. Compare with an in-turn release—Fig. 14.

the shoulders. The right shoulder is the fulcrum or hinge for the swing of the stone and any motion other than the natural elevation or lowering of the whole upper part of the body during the swing will alter the direction of that all-important line of delivery (see Fig. 9).

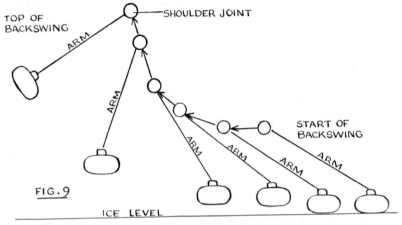

FIG. 9

The position of the head at the start of the delivery can be more easily illustrated than described. Figures 3 and 6 show the head erect, chin up and eyes looking straight ahead. In curling it is just as axiomatic to keep your eye on the skip's broom as it is to keep your eye on the ball during a golf swing. Any movement of the eyes unconsciously affects the movement of other muscles in the body.

Now that the position of the various parts of the body has been ascertained, let us get the stone in its proper place ready for delivery.

The position of the stone in taking the stance is so grossly misinterpreted by curlers and rule books alike that its importance cannot be over-emphasized. Contrary to popular belief, the only time the stone is placed on the centre line at the commencement of the lelivery is when the skip at the other end of the sheet is giving centre ice, i.e., he is holding his broom *on* the centre line. If he is asking the player for an out-turn and giving ice (holding his broom) say three feet to the left of the centre line (viz: to the left of the skip or to the right of the player in the hack) it is absolutely impossible to secure a true backswing along the correct line of delivery if the stone is placed on the centre line at the commencement of the back-swing. A simple application of lineal geometry will acquaint any doubter of this fact. Observe the diagrams below and draw your own conclusions.

The reverse naturally holds true in the case of an in-turn being played (to the skip's right or the player's left) off the centre line. The farther the skip's broom is from the centre line the more the player's stone is moved away from centre on that line. It is true

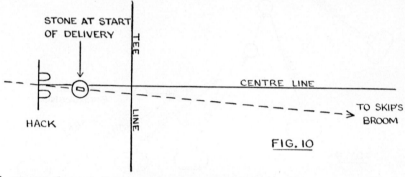

FIG. 10

that a good part of the stone will still be over (or on) the centre line no matter how much ice is given by the skip, but it is a common fallacy to assume that the stone must split that line at the commencement of the delivery on each and every shot.

I must confess that up to a few years ago I often had difficulty in "hitting" the broom accurately with my in-turn shots. Inevitably I was always a little narrow, and often I found myself "hooking" in-turn deliveries to try to correct the fault. It was not until I was trying to help a fellow curler straighten out his in-turn, which was always wide of the broom, that I suddenly realized the importance of the position of the stone at the start of the delivery as being the determining factor in being able to "split the broom" with all deliveries. I may as well confess that I was able to straighten out my friend in this regard but it didn't occur to me till a month later that I could profit from my own teachings, and try the idea myself. Strange to say, since then my in-turns have never caused my third man so much worry.

The Grip (See Fig. 12)

The different methods of grasping the handle of the stone and the different positions of the handle of the stone at the start of the

ENLARGEMENT OF DELIVERY AREA

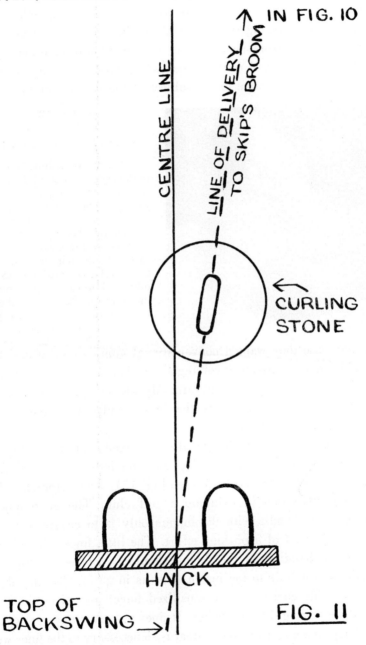

FIG. 11

delivery have always been the cause of much discussion among curlers as to which is right and which is wrong. Many times while sitting in the hack surrounded by a group of high-school boys interested in learning something about the rudiments of curling, a few adult onlookers peering over the heads and shoulders of the students could never restrain themselves from breaking in on my comments when I came to the subject of the position of the handle.

Fig. 12

GRIP—IN-TURN (from left)

The handle is inclined about 10° to the right of centre line and rests between the second and third joints of the fingers. The thumb rests lightly on the upper side of the handle. The palm of the hand is closer to the handle than is the case with the out-turn, because of their relative position to each other. However, at no time does the palm or the heel of the hand rest on the handle. See Fig. 6 for another view.

In each case they wanted conversational ammunition to add to the usual heated discussions involving a cross handle or a straight handle, particularly in case of the out-turn. My answer in all cases suggested the use of a grip that was the most comfortable and one that encouraged a free swing.

There is no doubt, though, that the handle of the stone should be grasped by the fingers only, with the index and third fingers applying most of the pressure (see Fig. 12). This resembles closely the grip advocated in swinging a golf club. The main object in gripping the handle with the fingers only is to ensure a swinging delivery instead of a pushing effort. The little finger should barely caress the handle and the thumb should be placed on top of the handle and a little to the inside (just as in golf). The thumb, with most notable curlers, is the sensitized finger and gives the feel of the stone during the backswing. It does not exert any real pressure but keeps the finger-tip control that is so necessary to the finer weight-shots such as draws, guards, or raises. The palm of the hand should never come into play, in fact the handle of the stone should lie across the fingers from the first joint on the little finger to the second joint on the index finger.

When the use of the fingers in the grip is mentioned, I do not mean the fingers enclosed in a heavy mitt or glove. The use of heavy mitts or gloves eliminates the feel of the handle that a player must have to be accurate. You will rarely see a top flight curler using heavy gloves any more than you would a golfer. True, in some climates in Western Canada, bare hands even in a few minutes, become numb with the cold. In such cases, a pair of light leather gloves should be worn (under heavy gloves or mitts) for use during delivery. Wool or cotton gloves of any thickness I have never found to be satisfactory in maintaining a light but firm grip. I have always been partial to light buckskin or deerskin gloves which I never shed while curling, no matter what the temperature level is. My fingers feel the handle through these gloves and there is sufficient friction from the leather to maintain a non-slip grip.

Fig. 13

GRIP—IN-TURN (from right)

The knuckles of the first three fingers should be visible to the player. Note the straight line from the end of the thumb back along the hand and the forearm. The thumb and fingers grasp the handle lightly but firmly.

Position of the Handle for In-Turn (See Figs. 12 and 13)

The most commonly accepted position of the handle at the start of the backswing for the delivery of an in-turn shot is what is known as the straight handle. That means the handle of the stone is parallel to the centre line with the goose-neck away from the player and the end of the handle nearest the hack. Many players, including myself, deviate slightly from this position. The end of the handle is pointed slightly outward (to the right) (see Fig. 13), to accommodate the natural hang of the right arm and right hand during the backswing. The physiology of the body must be considered in deciding on a correct position for the handle, because (and I apologize for repeating) every preparation for any movement to be made by the body must be such that during the mechanics of the swing, the bodily

Fig. 14

Ness Wise of Winnipeg illustrates the position of the handle of a stone at the moment of the release of an in-turn delivery. Note the handle easing out of the fingers of the right hand.

motions should be as effortless, as relaxed, as rhythmical and as natural as is humanly possible. Let your right arm hang loosely at your side, with the fingers of the hand closed lightly. Now reach forward slowly to a 45° position. Look at the exact position of your slightly closed hand. That should be the natural position at the start of the in-turn swing. The back of the hand and the four knuckles of the fingers are visible, and now if you turn your whole arm in (toward the body) until you can see the tips of your fingers you have completed the motion required for the delivery of an in-turn (see Fig. 14). Less than one-quarter turn of the wrist is necessary. There is no strain; no bending at the elbow, and no tightness at the shoulder. It is just as simple as that.

Position of the Handle for the Out-Turn (See Figs. 15A, B, C)

For the out-turn just reverse the procedure described above. Extend your arm and turn the arm in so that the tips of the fingers and the heel of the hand are visible. No tightening. Turn to this position without tensing a muscle, just as far as it will go without exerting any pressure. Now fit the handle of the stone into your lightly closed fingers and that should be a normal position for the start of an out-turn. Many A-1 curlers start the out-turn with a straight handle. My observation has been that such curlers are accurate fast-shot players. In any event use the method that comes most naturally and causes the least distortion of the muscles of the wrist, arm, and elbow. Use a grip for either in-turn or out-turn that allows a free and easy swing.

Amount of Turn or Spin Required

The greater the spin put on a stone when it is delivered, the less it will curl and the farther it will travel. Normally a stone handle should turn no more than twice or three times during its course to the other end of the ice. Spinners that rotate many times are difficult to gauge for weight and direction. A spinner on normal ice will draw only half as much as a rock with an average turning motion in the case of a hack weight shot for the simple reason that there is little chance for "cup-suction" with a "spinner". Many a skip has cursed to high heaven after he missed a take-out because he knew he had played the same weight and the same ice as his opponent yet he had missed the shot. He blamed the ice, a straw, his stone, or anything he could think of but he failed to realize that he had put more spin on his stone than his opponent had. Games are won and lost on this little oversight or lack of observation.

As a matter of fact, if a player by constant practice could become so proficient that he could put various amounts of spin on a stone and still be accurate, he could become the Joe Kirkwood of curling. Yet strange as it may sound no curler has exactly the same amount of spin on his out-turn as he has on his in-turn. This means that if you throw an in-turn shot with more spin than an out-turn you should take less ice for in-turn take-outs. So watch the spin you impart to the handle for each turn and judge your ice accordingly.

Fig. 15A

OUT-TURN GRIP (from left)

The handle is placed at a 60° angle to the centre line with the thumb pressing lightly on top. Only the second and third joints of the fingers come into contact with the handle. This allows the stone to hang on the fingers during the swing.

Fig. 15B

OUT-TURN GRIP (from right)

Finger-tip control is again evident in this view.

Fig. 15C

OUT-TURN GRIP (straight handle)

Several outstanding curlers start an out-turn delivery with the handle almost parallel to the centre line. The position of the fingers on the handle in this grip is similar to that used with the in-turn because the end of the handle is closer to the body.

Straight handles, or stones without a turn, cause grey hairs on any skip's head, not to mention the chagrin of the guilty player. Most straight handles are caused by imparting the turn to the handle too soon on the forward swing so that the handle is stationary as it leaves the fingers. This is one of the unforgivable sins in curling. Two or three straight handles a season are forgivable but two or three a game will certainly loosen the floodgates of any skip's vocabulary of not-too-well-chosen epithets.

The Back Swing (See Figs. 16 to 31)

Now we come to the most important part of the delivery—a correct back swing. I have already stressed that the prime object in a well-co-ordinated delivery is to use a stance that will enable a free and easy swing along the line of delivery. By the line of delivery I mean the imaginary line from the point of delivery to the skip's broom that you are aiming at, at the other end of the ice. A true back swing, then, must be a perfect extension of this line from the point where the delivery is started to a point at the top of the backswing. Anything that causes a wavering from this extended line will affect the direction of the stone in delivery. The diagrams below clearly illustrate this point.

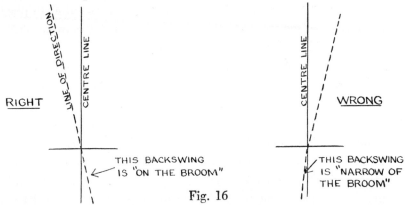

Fig. 16

Now that the object of the backswing is clear, let us examine the mechanics of achieving the desired result.

From the stance position, and with most of your weight on the right foot, draw your stone back with your fingers, straighten your right knee which will elevate your body and at the same time move your left foot back and possibly a little sideways in perfect synchronization with your right arm. During this motion the trunk, shoulders, and head are elevated by the straightening of the right knee but all three retain the same relative position to each other. There is no turning, twisting, or sagging. The shoulders are still square with the sheet in front; the head remains erect with the eyes focused constantly on the skip's broom (see Figs. 17 to 28). The stone during these movements hangs like a pendulum from the fingers of the right hand, with the right shoulder acting as the fulcrum or pivot during the swing. Imagine that you have hold of the handle of a pail of water and that you are swinging it backwards preparatory to swinging it forward and away from you. Then you have the feeling of the pendulum swing with a curling stone. Or, better still, imagine that you are playing a game of quoits with a small pail of sand for delivery instead of the quoit. Swing the pail back, then swing it forward and out. The weight of a stone requires good footing for the right foot and perfect balance. It takes some practice but it isn't long before you will feel perfectly at home in the hack.

At the start of the backswing, there is no need to push your stone farther forward as many players do after taking the stance in the hack (see Fig. 29). Some curlers even go so far forward as to place the right knee on the ice, as if they want to get as close to the skip's broom as possible before starting on their long return journey to the top of the backswing. In the first place such preliminary reaching, swaying, or stone-waggling is a waste of energy, and secondly, and more important, such unnecessary salutations are inclined to get the stone off the line of delivery. The short compact backswing starting from the stance position allows for the least possible margin of error.

I have often been asked, "Does the handle of the stone change its position during the backswing?" The answer is no, or very little, if any. The only reason for a change in the position of the handle would be to release any discomfort to the right arm, which is caused at times when a player uses a cross handle delivery with an out-turn. The obvious answer to any question of this kind is, "Let the arm act naturally during the swing". Don't try to force it into an uncomfortable position.

Fig. 17 — START OF THE BACKSWING (right side)

The straightening of the knees and resultant elevation of the hips have drawn the stone back from the stance position. (Compare with Fig. 3.) The left foot has not yet moved.

Fig. 18 — BACKSWING

The straightening of the right knee with consequent elevation of the body has drawn the stone back and above the ice. The slope of the back is more accentuated during this part of the backswing. The left foot has started moving back in symmetry with the stone. Note that through all the motions of the backswing, the head does not move.

Fig. 19 — BACKSWING

The trunk of the body is more erect at this stage of the backswing. The right arm is still straight and the body remains facing squarely up the ice.

Fig. 20 — BACKSWING

Here is an excellent photograph of the suspended action at the top of the backswing. Note the position of the stone. It seems to be barely hanging onto the fingers of the right hand, and illustrates forcefully the pendulum nature of the swing. Even the weight of a 42 lb. stone has failed to twist the shoulders or body off line in this pendulum swing. The ball and socket joint of the right shoulder acts as the fulcrum from which the right arm swings loosely. Notice the co-ordination between the right arm and left leg. The right knee has begun to bend and the whole body leans forward against the weight of the stone at the top of its backward swing, in preparation for the forward swing.

Fig. 21 — BACKSWING (left side)

The stone has been drawn back 12 to 14 inches from the stance position by straightening the knees and elevating the hips. Note the elevation of the hips in contrast to that of the shoulders and compare with Fig. 4. The left foot has not moved and the left arm and broom have been slightly elevated by the straightening of the knees.

Fig. 22 — BACKSWING

The left knee now is almost straight as the stone moves past the right leg and the left foot is ready to move back with the stone. The trunk of the body is more vertical as the body begins to straighten up. The left arm and hand remain in the same relative position.

Fig. 23 — BACKSWING

The lateral position of the left arm remains the same. The left leg is back and fully extended as the stone nears the top of the backswing. The body is even more erect.

Fig. 24 — BACKSWING

The momentum of the backward movement of the stone has caused the left arm to press back a bit to counterbalance this motion. The left leg and foot remain in the same positions but the body has reached its most erect position.

Fig. 25

BACKSWING (front view)

From the stance position (Fig. 6) the backswing commences by straightening the knees and raising the hips. This is the first conscious movement. The stone is pulled back by the fingers only because the right shoulder is elevated by the straightening of the knees. The right arm is relaxed and the rock hangs like a pendulum on the end of the fingers. Note the feet have not changed position at this stage. The head is still erect with the eyes focused ahead.

Fig. 26

BACKSWING

The left foot now synchronizes with the position of the stone and moves back in harmony acting as a counter-balance against the weight of the rock by moving back and out to the left at a 45° angle. The trunk of the body is now elevated and has lifted the stone above the ice. The head and eyes remain unchanged.

Fig. 27

BACKSWING

The left foot and the stone have moved well back. The body is fully elevated with shoulders, hips and trunk squarely facing the sheet of ice. The right knee is still partly flexed with almost the entire weight of the body pivoting on the right foot. Note the handle of the stone has not changed from its position at the start of the backswing.

Fig. 28

TOP OF THE BACKSWING

This is the moment of arrested motion of the body in order to check the momentum of the stone. The body actually commences its forward motion before the stone reaches the top of its arc in the swing. In the photo, note that the trunk of the body has started to lean forward almost hiding the stone in its position at the top of the swing.

Fig. 29 — BACKSWING

The above illustrates a position from which many players start their back-swing. It causes waste of unnecessary energy and allows too much margin for error in obtaining a backswing along the correct line of delivery. Compare this with the compact stance shown in Fig. 3.

The length of the backswing depends entirely on the amount of weight you want to play. A fast running shot would require a longer arc in the swing than a draw shot. In other words, if the proper weight is not given in the backswing it would have to be added in the forward swing or in the release of the stone, by means of a push. This is the very thing good curlers try to avoid because a push of any kind tends to throw the stone off the "line of delivery" which is so important. The purpose of the swing delivery is to eliminate any tendency to push the stone. Woe betide the pusher! The bitter pangs of remorse assail him often.

Practice will eventually give you the feel of weight that you want at the top of the backswing. In the meantime you will be getting the direction more consistently. A perfect weight player takes years to develop, just as it took Ben Hogan long, tedious hours of practice trying to hit a golf ball to the spot where he wanted it.

The Forward Swing (See Figs. 30 to 41)

The forward swing is really the backswing in reverse. The right arm has reached the top of its pendulum with the stone hanging from the fingers. The weight of the stone now starts the right arm swinging forward and now is the time to start giving the turn to the handle. Don't consciously turn the wrist, rather turn the whole arm in (for an in-turn) or out (for an out-turn) so that the handle is turning as you release the stone. Do not wait until near the end of the forward swing to give the turn to the handle as the pressure exerted in the short distance to go will affect the line of the swing. If the handle is not turning as you let the stone go, you will have to give it a turn or twist after the stone is on the ice. Thus a push or hook delivery is inevitable and too often the direction of the stone is changed. (That is always the cue for the skip to throw up his arms and turn his back in disgust.)

Above all else, keep the right arm straight in the forward swing and if you let the stone hang on your fingers and keep the palm of the hand away from the handle, your arm cannot bend because you have swung the stone completely through and out in front of you. Similarly, if you swing the stone on your fingers it will always be ahead of your body when it hits the ice and you will not be able to develop a push delivery. No matter whether you deliver from the hack without any slide, swing the stone cleanly towards the broom. A true sliding delivery follows the same tactics and the slide occurs after the swing at the broom.

Balance and Co-ordination During the Forward Swing

A perfectly executed forward swing will give you the feeling of good balance and effortless rhythm. The forward motion of the body and the release of the stone should be as smooth and unhurried as the flow of cream from a jug. Many hours of practice are necessary to achieve the delightful "feel" of having acquired perfect co-ordination.

The right foot is the sure yet flexible pivot of the swing. The weight of the stone suspended from the right hand and arm is delicately balanced by the caressing motion of a partly extended left foot moving forward in unison with the right arm and the extended left arm with broom in hand, which will sway slightly backward and forward to maintain the equilibrium of the shoulders and head. If the arms and legs move in complete harmony with each other during the swing, the trunk, shoulders and head will never alter their relative position to each other. The perfect alignment of these parts all through the mechanics of the swing is vitally necessary to a true

Fig. 30 — FORWARD SWING

The forward swing has just commenced. The right knee is bending and the trunk is moving forward and down. (Compare with Fig. 20.) The left leg is ready to move forward with the swing of the stone. The handle of the stone has not yet begun to turn.

Fig. 31 — FORWARD SWING

The downward swing of the stone finds the body well-inclined. Note the left foot commencing to swing forward with the stone. Head is erect, and there is no twisting of the body. The stone is hanging loosely at the end of a relaxed right arm.

Fig. 32 — FORWARD SWING

The stone is about to hit the ice cleanly and the body weight is about to shift to the left foot. The right arm begins to turn at this point to give the in-turn to the handle. (Note: All illustrations with the exception of those specifically mentioned show an in-turn delivery.)

Fig. 33 — FORWARD SWING

The handle of the stone is being released. This photograph illustrates the first part of the follow-through rather than the last part of the forward swing. Note the extended right leg and right arm.

Fig. 34 — START OF THE FORWARD SWING

The body makes the first forward motion. (Compare with Fig. 24.) The left leg reaches well back, and the left arm (broom in hand) is fully extended at right angles. The stone actually reaches the top of its arc at this stage. Note unchanged position of hips and shoulders, both squarely facing the line of delivery.

Fig. 35 — FORWARD SWING

From position in Fig. 34, the stone and left foot have moved forward simultaneously, with the stone always slightly ahead of the left foot during the swing forward. The body is lower and more inclined.

Fig. 36 — FORWARD SWING

The stone has reached the ice surface. The momentum of the forward swing has pulled the left arm back slightly to help keep balance. The right leg is straightening out. (In the case of a long slide it snaps straight and gives the necessary leg drive from the hack.)

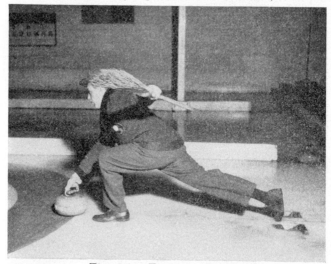

Fig. 37 — FORWARD SWING

The left knee has bent to allow the body to lower itself even more. The left arm is fairly well back in this photograph to offset the forward reach of the right arm. (Note in Fig. 42—the left arm has readjusted its position during the follow-through.) The stone is well ahead of the body, illustrating the stretch-out and reach-out-after feeling that a player should have just before the release.

Fig. 38

FORWARD SWING (front view)

The stone has started its return to the ice and the trunk of the body is pitched well forward and is being lowered with the stone. The left foot has barely commenced its forward motion.

Fig. 39 — FORWARD SWING

The forward swing has begun. The left foot is moving forward with the stone. The right shoulder has dropped slightly because of the weight of the rock, but the hips and chest are facing the sheet squarely and the eyes are focused intently on the line of delivery.

Fig. 40 — Forward Swing

The turn is now being imparted to the handle. (So little turn is necessary that it is difficult to detect this motion.) Note the looseness of the right arm and hand, and the position of both knees pointing straight ahead.

Fig. 41 — Forward Swing

The forward swing has been completed and the stone is leaving the hand. The fingers of the hand have merely opened to release the handle which you will notice has rotated only an inch or so at this point. The stone is well in front of the body and although a true slider will travel many feet after the stone, he has lost control of the rock at this point.

swing along the line of delivery. A study of all figures illustrating
the swing will furnish practical evidence.

The Follow-Through

When Joe DiMaggio hits a home run, the moment his bat connects
with the ball the damage is done, the follow-through of his bat is
physically unnecessary to the flight of the ball. Why waste this
extra energy? Simply because the nerve impulses from the brain to
the muscles are too slow to check the movement of the bat immediately
after impact. Similarly, if the mind is conscious of a follow-through
being unnecessary, the muscular reflexes may act too soon, and
unconsciously the arc of the swing is disturbed before impact.
Because of the comparative time gap between muscular reaction and
impulses from the brain, top-notch performers in all sports concentrate on a follow-through to a point well beyond the required point
of impact or delivery. And this exaggeration of the motion required
gives the player smooth, unhesitating, and uninterrupted rhythm of
motion.

The delivery of a stone in curling offers no exception to this rule.
The follow-through occurs after the stone has left the hand and a
player should be conscious of attempting the follow-through during
the entire forward swing. Don't wait till after the stone has left the
hand. Think of it as you are swinging the stone towards the broom.
Whether you deliver from the hack, whether you use a short slide or
a long slide, is immaterial. With your eyes constantly on the skip's
broom, your right arm reaches forward and follows the stone along
the line of its direction, while the fingers of the right hand release
the handle and in so doing almost consciously try to reach out-and-
after the stone, so that even after the rock is ten feet out ahead of
you, your right arm, hand, and fingers are pointing along the path
the stone is travelling toward the broom (see Fig. 42). Make it a
habit to do this continually and not only will your delivery be more
accurate but you'll know, too, whether your skip is right when he
roars out, "You're wide!" "You're narrow!" Incidentally you can
tell within a very few inches, how accurate your delivery is by
sighting with your eye along the right arm, hand, and fingers, through
the handle of your stone to the skip's broom. The closer your body

Fig. 42 — The Sliding Follow-Through

This photograph was taken early in the season with resulting evidence of inflexibility. Normally the body is lower by virtue of sliding on the ball of the left foot instead of the flat of the foot as illustrated.

Fig. 43 — The Sliding Follow-Through

The sliding follow-through from this angle shows the handle of the stone, fingers of the right hand, and the right eye perfectly lined up on the broom. In mid-season the body is even lower and the player may get the same feeling as a marksman sighting along the barrel of a gun.

is to the ice at the time of sighting, the easier it will be to gauge your line to the broom. This is one of the advantages of the sliding delivery (see Fig. 43).

Faults to Avoid in the Follow-through

1. Pushing with the palm, or fingers. This is a sign that there was insufficient backswing if the push was to add weight; or if it was for the purpose of correcting your direction, it simply means that your swing was not along the proper line of direction.

2. Jumping to an erect position as soon as the stone leaves the fingers. This habit alone causes many "off the broom" deliveries. The follow-through is non-existent. The weight is often disturbed by such precipitate action, and it's impossible for the player to tell accurately whether he was "on" the broom.

3. Running after the stone to sweep it. Why not concentrate on the delivery so that the stone has the correct weight when it leaves the hand? A player should not move from his follow-through position until the stone is at least twenty feet away from him. This is exactly the same fault as looking up in a golf swing. Keep your eye on the broom!

4. A flourishing movement of the hand after releasing the handle. This may give the player a feeling of gracefulness but it doesn't help the direction of the stone. More often a hand flying up will brush the handle and change the direction of the stone or cause a change in the turn of the handle. Such motions disturb the follow-through which should be a "reach-after" motion.

5. Allowing the body to drift sideways or swivel after the release of the stone. This fault is common amongst "sliders" and will be dealt with later.

CHAPTER 2

The Sliding Delivery

Tempers have often risen to the boiling point when curlers get into controversial arguments over the use of the sliding delivery. As my name has been associated constantly with this oft-maligned style, it is only fitting that I make some sort of attempt in these pages to defend its use and clear up many misunderstandings.

Objections to the Sliding Delivery

At the present moment, I believe that Manitoba is the only province in Canada that has not legislated against the long slide in its rule books. However, I stand to be corrected. Most other Curling Associations definitely state in their rules that the player "must release the handle of the stone before the stone is clearly over the sweeping score drawn across the tee." This is a plain directive that leaves no doubt as to its meaning. The agitators in favour of this rule and their spokesmen at Association meetings were emphatic about their objections to any player using a long slide for several reasons. To their mind it was an unfair, and therefore illegal, delivery because they firmly believed it was possible for a player with a long slide to secure advantage over those who did not use it, in two ways:

1. By delivering the stone at the end of a long slide, a player could be more accurate in delivery by virtue of being closer to the broom when he released the stone.

2. By sliding out at an angle from the hack, a player could obtain unfair advantage by directing his stone around a guard. In other words, if a player pushed off from the hack at a twenty or thirty degree angle, he could conceivably deliver the stone at the end of his slide (which might be four feet to the left of the centre line) where he could easily see a well-guarded stone to pass it through; or, similarly, he could bury his rock behind a guard so well that his

opponent couldn't come anywhere near it with a stone delivered in the normal manner.

Personally, I fully agree that such achievements are entirely within the realm of possibility, but for a player to be able to do this consistently is highly improbable. Furthermore, I have never yet in my thirty years of experience tried to perform this extraordinary feat nor have I seen any curler deliberately effect the miracle of negotiating a guard in this manner. True I have often seen sliders who drift off line in their delivery unconsciously; or, if consciously, they wonder why they are doing it and try to correct it, usually with calamitous results. In such cases, I feel sorry for the poor skip who calculates the ice required to play a certain shot and then is left scratching his head in consternation when his second man, with the drifting slide delivery, apparently gets the broom but (inevitably) misses the shot. I myself have had enough worries in this respect to agitate my duodenal ulcer to earthquake dimensions. Two of our "leads" during the past few years have been cursed with this disease, and even after long hours of coaching and attempted remedies when they had obtained temporary relief, the accursed drift would manifest itself again and again, and usually at a crucial point in the game when a miss had me groping for the aspirin jar. But let me leave the causes and effects of this nightmare of all sliders for later discussion.

The objection of many curlers to the delivery of the stone at the end of a long slide has some ground for consideration. The objectors refer, of course, to a slider riding his stone up the ice (in some cases as far as the hog line) before releasing it with a push delivery. Not only does it confound the original intention of a proper curling delivery (see Fig. 44), but it is as unrhythmical and unco-ordinated a pose as can be seen on any curling ice. Those whose ire is aroused to combustible proportions by such antics may take some solace in the knowledge that no curler of championship calibre will be developed with the aid of this unusual delivery. Please remember that I differentiate between the individual who rides out on his stone (i.e. with the rock almost under him) and the one who slides out after his stone with his right arm extended ahead of him at full length and therefore is following his stone. The former is a "riding pusher"

Fig. 44

THE FOLLOW-THROUGH

Note the raised left heel, and the slide on the left toe. The slide usually terminates two or three feet in front of the rings.

Photo courtesy Don Dunbar
Inco Triangle

and the latter a "swinging slider". The rider thinks that he is copying the sliding delivery, but in reality he has developed a cross between ice-sailing and shuffleboard.

Time and again I have had the blame for this hybrid delivery placed squarely on my shoulders. One of my own clubmates who is noted for his candid expressions of opinion, said to me during a locker-room post-mortem: "Watson, you have done a lot to interest young people in curling, but your d —— d slide has ruined more curlers than it has helped". There is more truth than fiction in that accusation. Young curlers, particularly boys, are fascinated by the slide and attempt to copy it. In many cases, lack of proper observation, or teaching, or lack of the chance to observe, or trying to slide by imitating a curler who is a "rider", causes a great conglomeration of assorted sliding, riding, and gliding tactics, any and all of which are designated by the term "sliding delivery". If I have been inadvertently the cause of much of this confusion, here is an opportunity to put the records straight once and for all. If you who peruse these pages will pass the information on to the would-be sliders, you will help them to understand the true mechanics of the sliding delivery and thereby improve their effectiveness as well as the dispositions of those they play with and against.

As to how curling legislators and rule makers should handle this contentious matter, may I offer my suggestions for what they may be worth? In the first place, to the objection that the long slide is unfair and therefore illegal, I reiterate that a slider who drifts to one side or deliberately tries to slide at an angle will cause so much havoc to his own delivery and give his skip so many headaches in calculating ice for him that any occasional advantage gained would be offset by too great a percentage of misses on simple shots. Personally, if I knew an opponent was deliberately trying to make such a shot I would be inwardly pleased, for his chances of making it would be slim, and in a close match it would mean a shot wasted that might have been used to better advantage. So in this respect any rule restricting the length of the slide is making a mountain out of a molehill and is inviting friction and ill-feeling between players that is definitely foreign to the usual goodwill that exists in the curling fraternity.

The second objection, to the "rider" who delivers beyond the tee line at the end of his ride, can be dismissed similarly, for a pusher never gets the broom consistently, and he would be well advised to learn the mechanics of a good swing delivery if he is anxious to become a better curler. Any curlers who worry about such unorthodox methods should feel sorry for such misguided individuals, for they are due for many tribulations as a result of worrying about their "misses".

As for the long sliders who use a strong "push off" from the hack, I have only one suggestion to make. Eliminate the restricted sliding rule and replace it with the following: "Once the player has left the hack in making delivery of his stone, said stone should be considered as played and may not be brought back to the hack for another delivery." This would offset the only advantage a slider possesses under prevailing rules. If he loses balance during the slide he cannot then hang on to the stone and go back to the hack for another try. That will stop many of the "riders", but it will not often affect a true "swing-slide" delivery.

The long slide has several disadvantages that many players are not aware of:

1. Once you get past age 45 the joints of the body are not as flexible as they used to be and there will be more creaking and groaning in your attempts to flatten out your body behind the stone.

2. Once you get past a slim 36 waistline you will experience the same difficulty.

3. On wet or swingy ice you will be under a terrific handicap unless you learn to swing from the hack.

4. On badly chipped ice in front of the hack you will experience rough sliding on occasions.

5. On side ice, i.e., on ice sloping to right or left along the line of delivery, you'll find your stone slipping sideways out of your fingers. Let me tell you—it is a helpless feeling.

So don't resent the long sliders. They have plenty of troubles of their own. Don't discourage a delivery that is attracting thousands to the game as participants and as spectators. Rather encourage the youngsters or the newcomer to learn the basis of a good swing first, before he attempts the sliding follow-through.

Curling to-day has become a spectator sport. The long slide, perfectly executed, has added colour to the game and interested thousands. Let us not clutter our rule books with fettering regulations that will stagnate the progress that has been made. Let us follow-through in expanding our great fraternity to include the fellowship of thousands of youngsters who are fascinated by the swinging slide delivery and the sociability and competitiveness of the roaring game. Make no mistake about it. The slide has come to stay or we shall give the game back to our grandfathers.

How the Slide Developed

It will be much easier to understand the mechanics of a well-synchronized slide delivery if the story of its evolution is told first.

The birth of the hack in curling made sliding possible. The old Scotch "crampit", which is still in use in some parts of Scotland, was a flat steel or iron plate similar in dimension to the "mat" used by lawn bowlers and as there was no opportunity for a toe-hold of any kind, it was imperative that the stone be delivered from a standing crouch position. The weight of a curling stone made it well nigh impossible to face the sheet squarely when delivering, thus the crouch stance with side-arm delivery was commonplace. Very rarely would a player take a step forward from the crampit to help synchronize the body movements while swinging the stone forward. The under-footing was too precarious to risk a bad fall to the ice. But with the advent of the hack a new era developed. The hack allowed a toe-hold. Now the player could swing freely, and with sure-footing began to throw faster rocks. The draw game gave way slowly to "chap and lie", and in some areas the "running game" became popular. Indirectly, when a curler began throwing faster stones the first indications of the slide were noticeable as the greater arc of the stone, the weight of the stone, and the follow-through pulled him out of the hack even if only a foot or so. If he wore rubbers or overshoes, which he did, the flat of the sole of the rubber on the left foot caused enough friction to make the slide very short. Such was the case with the famous Bob Dunbar of the early 1900's. He had a smooth, rhythmic swing and, according to tales of his prowess, he was the deadliest sharpshooter of them all. His running shots "smacked" opposition rocks with unerring accuracy. His secret was his perfect balance and follow-through which he practised by the hour. His follow-through only took him two or three feet out in front of the hack.

Then along came Frank Cassidy, another name to conjure with in Western curling annals. Reportedly, Cassidy's swing was a pleasure to watch. His perfect symmetry of motion drew admiring comments wherever he curled. Spectators noticed that he went further out from the hack in his follow-through than did Dunbar. In fact, he slid out on the side of his left foot an unbelievable distance to a point anywhere between the back of the eight-foot or twelve-foot ring. Cassidy had found that by such a delivery he could flatten out the arc of his swing and concentrate on throwing his whole body towards the broom.

About 1913, a youngster named Gordon Hudson, started curlers' tongues wagging, and during the span of the next twenty years, the name Hudson brought dismay to those drawn against him. Here was a curler who out-Cassidyed Cassidy in his follow-through slide.

By using his heel and the side of his left foot he could "glide" to the front ring with his sliding delivery. Along about the 1920's Gordon Hudson's name and style was a byword to those of us who, as youngsters, loved to curl. We watched his every delivery and every move. We even imitated his mannerisms and his gestures. But his slide we couldn't imitate. All of us on our kid rink (averaging 18 years of age) were slim in build. Our ankles weren't strong enough to support a "side-of-the-foot" or "heel" delivery. Constant hours

Fig. 45 — LEG DRIVE

Grant Watson uses a powerful leg drive to obtain his long slide. The photograph shows both him and the stone still travelling at the same speed even though he has not released the handle at the front rings. This type of slide is difficult to perfect for the player usually develops a tendency to drift.

of practice failed to develop his slide for us. Then one night near midnight, after the evening games had been concluded, the four of us were out practising as usual when, to our amazement, Alex Chalmers, our lead, went skidding out crazily after a stone which he was delivering and ended up flat on his face somewhere near the hog line. The idea was born. Remove the left rubber and, presto! we could slide even further than the Great Gordon Hudson. What a thrill it was during the balance of that winter trying to keep balance and get the nose down to the handle of the stone at the same time!

It seemed only natural to suppose that, by getting the eye immediately behind the extended right arm and hand and looking through the handle of the stone toward the broom at the other end, our marksmanship would be more accurate. It was just like sighting down a gun barrel. Believe me, it worked. The following year, 1926, we astounded ourselves more than anyone else in winning the Walker Theatre trophy in the world's largest bonspiel (Winnipeg).

Fortunately for us, as the experience of later years proved, we had curled for three years before the amazing discovery of a "rubberless" slide. During those years we had developed a true basic swing so that the slide became only an exaggerated follow-through. Here is the mistake made by too many young curlers: they want to practise the slide first, so they never develop the swing along the line of direction. *In the true sliding delivery, the stone is swung at the broom from the hack, and the slide simply follows the direction of the stone.* The two together are synchronized into a smooth-flowing, effortless motion.

The Mechanics of a Sliding Delivery

The only difference between a swing delivery and a swing-slide delivery exists in the mechanics of the forward swing. The stance, grip, and backswing are identical for both deliveries. The forward swing in both cases is exactly the same with only two points of difference. These affect the use of (a) the right leg, (b) the left foot.

The Right Leg

The length of the slide is determined by the force exerted by the right foot and leg in the drive or push off from the hack, and the way the left foot is used during the slide. Long sliders snap the right knee straight during the forward swing by pressing hard with the ball of the foot against the back of the hack. This action produces a powerful drive with the right leg that propels the player out of the hack so that he is travelling at the same speed as the stone during the early part of the follow-through (see Fig. 45).

The Left Foot

During such a delivery, the length of the follow-through, or slide, depends almost entirely on the friction offered by the left foot to the ice surface. This foot bears the entire weight of the body once

Fig. 46

EFFECT OF CREPE-SOLED SHOES

The famous Jimmy Welsh of Deer Lodge Club, Winnipeg, uses a short slide because he uses crepe-soled shoes and slides on the flat of his left foot. Jimmy is deadly accurate with his fast-running shots.

Fig. 47 — MEDIUM SLIDE

Gordon Hudson, twice Canadian Champion, is noted for his medium slide on the side of the left rubber, as well as for a turned-in right foot that acts as a rudder to keep his body directly in line behind the stone during delivery.

Fig. 48 — Medium Slide

Alex Welsh, brother of Jimmy, uses a medium-length slide, by using more leg drive from the hack. If he wore leather soles instead of crepe-rubber his slide would be similar in length to my own. Note his extended right leg and the position of the right toe.

the player leaves the hack. There are several ways of sliding on the left foot. I will deal with them in order of the length of slide provided.

1.   The short slide:

When a rubber or overshoe is worn and the slide is on the flat of the foot, a short slide will result (see Fig. 46).

2. (a)   The medium slide:

When a player slides on the heel of his left rubber or on the side of the left foot, less friction is offered by the ice and a slide of medium length to the tee line or front ring is the result (see Fig. 47).

2. (b)   Another medium slide:

Jimmy Welsh and his famous rink wear crepe-soled shoes without rubbers. Thus they have developed a middle length slide which is executed mostly on the flat of the foot (see Fig. 48).

Still another fad at present in use by some curlers is the use of shoes with a felt sole to accomplish the follow-through.

3.   The long slide:

The so-called "Watson slide" which terminates about half way between the front ring and the hog line (depending on the condition of the ice surface) is accomplished by removing the rubber from the left foot and sliding on the ball of the foot. The leather on a thin-soled shoe offers little resistance to the ice surface and as a result the follow-through with the slide carries the player a long way past the point where he has released the handle of the stone.

Many arguments have centred around the question of where I release the stone, and I have been called to the phone at 2:00 A.M. to settle the question so that a bet could be collected promptly. But I doubt if any of these arguments have been settled satisfactorily to all concerned because there is no one specified answer to the question.

A news reporter once insisted on a photograph being taken to squelch the squear , once and for all. As a matter of fact, the photograph showed t I had released the handle of the stone before crossing the tee lin   it it did not reveal that the stone in question failed to reach the farther hog-line. Nor could any individual observation prove the point conclusively.

The point at which the stone leaves the hand will vary according to: (1) The condition of the ice surface, (2) The length of the backswing, (3) The amount of force exerted in the push off from the hack.

The type of pebble used on ice affects the length of the slide considerably. A fine spray pebble offers little resistance to the left shoe and the slide will lengthen as the pebble wears off. The diamond or square pebble in vogue in Eastern Canada on artificial ice offers very little resistance to a leather "toe slide". As a result, in 1936 when the "Sliding Schoolteachers from Manitoba" (as we were known then) performed on the beautiful surface at the Granite Curling Club in Toronto, our slides were longer than ever and caused much head-shaking among the veteran curlers in attendance. Charlie Kerr, our lead on that occasion, used a slide delivery and as he was 6 feet 3 inches in height, by the time he stretched his long arm and body from the hack his stone had almost crossed the tee line before he even got out of the hack. So when the diamond pebble offered no resistance whatever to his slide, observers gaped unbelievingly when he got to his feet at the end of his follow-through three or four feel beyond the first hog line. With the spray pebble that he normally played on, he would not have coasted half that far, and he was as amazed as anyone. Frosty ice and wet ice have the opposite effect. They cut many feet off the slide.

The longer or higher the backswing the longer the slide. My brother Grant uses a much higher backswing than I do and there-

Fig. 49 — LEANING ON THE BROOM

A common fault in younger curlers is illustrated above. This young slider has leaned on the long straw of his broom to aid balance during the slide. This acts as a brake and pulls the body into the position above. The body should remain in a direct line behind the stone. (See Fig. 42.)

fore is a longer slider (see Fig. 45). He seems to be able to handle himself better by using a longer swing but I have seen many curlers who have tried to imitate him run into a lot of grief in doing so. Personally, I do not see any advantage in too long a slide. It has disadvantages similar to over-swinging in golf.

A combination of a high backswing and a strong push-off from the hack has an effect much like that achieved by jet-propelled aircraft on the take-off. Too many curlers seem to want to make a torpedo of their bodies, and with intense physical effort, hurl them-selves at the broom. Most of these individuals are the riders who push the rock towards the broom as soon as their momentum slows down to a near stop. To my mind, the more compact a swinging slide and follow-through are, the better the chance of flawless performance. The only valid reason for removing a rubber to aid the slide is to eliminate any sudden jarring to the motion of the body in completing the follow-through. It lends itself to natural symmetry, which is not found in a player who exaggerates his backswing and the drive from the hack.

Common Faults in the Sliding Delivery

In order to complete a description of the sliding delivery for any curler who is using this type of delivery or is interested in analyzing it or trying it, I shall try to attack the problems that confront the slider, by means of descriptions and illustrations of the position of various parts of the body during the execution of this type of delivery. Let me warn you again that there are so many variations of style and so many bad habits that you can unconsciously drift into, that to try copying this type of delivery will do many curlers a lot more harm than good. But if you are determined to slide, watch these points:

1. *The position of the left arm and the use of the broom*

If you examine Fig. 49, you will see one of our younger curlers in the act of a sliding delivery using his broom to lean on for balance. Fig. 53 shows what happens when the broom is used in this way. The friction of the broom straw has acted as a resisting fulcrum and pulled the whole body around at right angles to the sheet as the rock leaves the hand.

The body actually is turning before the release of the handle in such a case, and very often the line of direction of the stone is changed before the stone leaves the hand. In addition, it is very seldom that such a player knows how accurate he is in "hitting" the skip's broom, because he is not in a position to see after the stone leaves his hand.

Now look back at Fig. 42. The broom is on the ice to keep balance but it is sliding along with the player and does not pull him off the line of delivery.

2. *The position of the right leg*

During the slide the right leg and toe act as an anchor for the body. At all times it should be extended straight back with very little bend at the knee (see Fig. 50). This keeps the body low and well behind the stone so that the player can better see the line of delivery.

Fig. 50 — RIGHT TOE RUDDER

Bruce Hudson, a teen-age curler, demonstrates the fully-extended right leg and the turning in of the right toe to act as a rudder in keeping the body directly behind the stone when using the slide delivery.

Fig. 51

BALANCED SLIDE

Leo Johnson of Winnipeg, Canadian Championship Skip, 1933, demonstrates his colourful "balanced slide" delivery, which is difficult to master because of the elevated left arm. Leo has developed perfect balance and coordination in his graceful delivery motion.

Many sliders have trouble because they drift (usually to the right) while sliding. This is ordinarily due to one of three causes: (1) Arc of backswing is off line; (2) Body weight is unbalanced and leaning too much to the right; (3) The toe of the right foot points out too far and drags the body to the right. The first two can be corrected easily by conscious effort, but the last fault takes some practice to eliminate. The right toe should be turned in (see Fig. 51), and in such a position it will feel uncomfortable until much practice makes the movement natural. If you look again at Fig. 41, you will notice that my right toe is pointing out slightly, yet fortunately for me it has never given me any worry about drifting. No doubt I do drift occasionally because of the position of this toe, but the drift (which is little if any) takes place after the stone is well on its way. The long slider has too much chance to drift before releasing his stone and therefore tries to correct the line of delivery just before it leaves his hand. The result is that his stone comes toward the broom from another point on the ice, and the angle made is something like this:

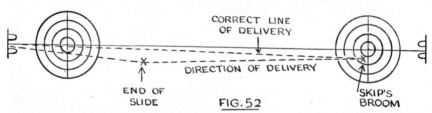

FIG. 52

This is the point that critics of the sliding delivery bring up as being unfair, but the poor suffering player who has missed many shots as a result of it, would gladly pay the same critics anything if they could only tell him how to get rid of it. The angle of direction to the broom is so different from the one intended that a hack-weight take-out on normal ice will miss by 1½ to 2 feet. Well, you might say, why doesn't the skip allow for this. I have. But on the next shot he doesn't drift so far and his rock comes at the broom from another angle. So what am I to do? A drifter really has his problems, and so has his skip (see Fig. 53).

3. *The "hook" delivery*

Most pushers are guilty of "hooking" their stone handles by

trying to correct the line of delivery at the end of the slide, but many swing sliders offend in this respect, too. The only reason a slider might have to do this is because his backswing is off line and as the stone is about to leave his hand he can see that he is going to be narrow or wide so he tries to correct his line by "hooking" the handle in or out. Watch the position of your stone at the start of the backswing and you will have no trouble. Drifting sliders, on the contrary, have no alternative but to "hook" or push.

Fig. 53 — DRIFTING SLIDE

Here Charlie Read illustrates how a drifting slide makes it necessary for the player to deliver his stone from a point outside the correct line of delivery. Note that the stone is moving toward the centre line to correct the off-line slide. With a normal slide Charlie's left foot should be no more than a few inches from the centre line.

4. *Taking the eye off the broom*

The longer the slide the more you must concentrate on keeping your eye on the broom. Many sliders unconsciously drop their gaze to the handle of the stone or even to the ice before the rock has left the hand. As in golf, your eye should be on the broom seconds after the stone handle has been released. Check yourself on this next time you play. You may be surprised.

To Slide or Not to Slide

If the foregoing pages of this chapter do nothing else, I sincerely hope they convince the player that the long slide is only a means to an end. It is not by any stretch of the imagination a necessity to good curling.

During the 1949 tour of the Scottish Curlers to this continent, I had the pleasure of playing against the visitors at the Strathcona Club in Winnipeg. John Monteith, Captain of the Scots number two team, was playing on the next sheet. His observations of my style of delivery were recounted to me later that evening. According to the report, Monteith turned to Jack Dutton who was playing against him, and nodding in my direction as I delivered a stone, he asked, "Who's that?" Dutton replied, "Oh, that's Ken Watson!" Whereupon the Scot said, "Aye, so that's Watson. I have heard a lot about him. I believe I have seen his picture in the papers. He must be quite a curler. But he'd no be allowed to curl in Scotland!" I took a ribbing on that one for weeks afterward. Oddly enough, though, it was scarcely a month later that Geo. Iliffe, The Strathcona Club President at that time, gave me a real thrill when he read a letter from John Monteith thanking the Club for the hospitality tendered his team and inviting members to join the Canadian Curlers tour to Scotland in 1950, even to the extent of including a fellow by the name of "Watson".

In any event, whether you favour a long slide, a short slide, or no slide at all, by all means use the method that is most comfortable to you and the one that gives you the best results. Fifteen years ago there were few exponents of the long slide, but after 1936 when a team of long sliders won the Canadian Curling Championship many thought that this type of delivery was primarily responsible. Thousands of players started removing the left rubber until loose rubbers and overshoes were strewn over ice lanes all across Canada. Even the brilliant Howard Wood, noted for his "stay-in-the-hack" delivery, removed his foot gear and slid out a foot or two. But too many curlers went to too great an extreme in their enthusiasm to acquire the slide, and over-exaggerated styles resulted. The long slide is not the answer to the dream of perfection in shotmaking. It is only the polished finish of a well-balanced swing. Learn the swing first before you think about the slide.

CHAPTER 3

More Ways To Better Curling

"Many are called but few are chosen", is an expression truly applicable in curling circles when it comes to selecting the personnel of a top-notch rink for competitive play. When an A-class skip is casting about for curlers to make up his rink, he will wisely look over the field of available material very carefully. No doubt he has had his eye on several individuals during the past season and he has mentally noted the qualifications he desires in any player whom he considers asking to play for him. Naturally, this hypothetical skip should have these qualifications himself if he is to be successful in getting his ideal rink together. (There have been skips who have had greater respect for their own prowess than others have had.) In any event, the question I am going to attempt to answer in this chapter is, "What abilities is a skip looking for in selecting a player for his rink?" or to be even more specific, "What abilities should a good skip look for in selecting the members of his rink?" No matter how careful he is in his selection, and no matter how accurate he is in his final analysis, he will never get the perfect curler because no such individual exists. But here to my mind is a short sketch of a skip's dream of a perfect curler.

QUALITIES DESIRED BY THE SKIP IN A CURLER

Physical Characteristics
1. A well-balanced and "grooved" swing delivery
2. A good sense of "weight"
3. Willingness to practise
4. A good sweeper
5. A good judge of ice
6. Ability to judge weight of a stone in sweeping
7. Experience and positions previously played

Mental and Spiritual Characteristics

The 7 C's for Success in Curling:

1. Compatability
2. Concentration
3. Co-operation
4. Courage
5. Confidence
6. Competitiveness
7. Consistency

Every curler has his weaknesses and you will seldom find a player who has more than seventy-five percent of the exacting qualifications demanded above. If you did, then you have unearthed a skip of championship calibre.

You might be interested to know which of the characteristics listed I would consider as the basic minimum requirements of a player before he can be considered potential material. Of the fourteen qualifications listed, here are the "Big Six":

1. Compatability
2. A good delivery
3. A good sense of weight
4. Competitiveness
5. Position previously played
6. Mental courage

It is comparatively easy to write in terms of generalities when referring to the qualities of a good curler, but I can assure you that the list above was not a hastily prepared one. It is a subject to which I have given considerable thought. I firmly believe that the mental and spiritual characteristics that I have enumerated are prerequisites for success in almost any field of endeavour. If those of you who have been devotees of the game of curling for a period of years will think back over the names of expert curlers you have played with or against, you cannot help coming to the same conclusion. Many of these qualities stands out clearly and unmistakably in any outstanding curler.

There is no need to digress further; I will attempt to give you my reasons why each and every characteristic named is important to better curling.

Physical Characteristics

Some of us have acquired or inherited natural co-ordination and others have not. I have noticed that baseball players, golfers, rugby players—in fact, participants in any other sport—"take" to curling more naturally than individuals who have had no previous athletic experience. To my mind this does not mean that there is no hope for the man or boy who is not athletically inclined, rather it will require more observation, practice, and concentration to equal the developed co-ordination of the others.

Starting young at the game is an invaluable aid. A boy of fifteen who practically grows up with a stone and a broom in his hand has a tremendous physical advantage in delivery over another who starts the game at thirty. That is one very good reason why the West has won the Canadian curling title on all but three occasions. We start them young in Western Canada. In my case, at age 45, when many men are just becoming interested in curling, I have had thirty years of curling experience behind me. This doesn't mean, naturally, that there is no hope if you start curling in your late thirties or forties, for I can name dozens of members of district and provincial championship rinks who have attained that eminence after five to ten years at the game.

Co-ordination is an important physical asset to any good curler, but it is not, in itself, the only requirement. Many curlers who lack rhythmic movement in delivery atone for it in other ways.

1. *A Well-Balanced and "Grooved" Swing Delivery*

As this has been dealt with in detail in Chapter 1 no further mention will be necessary.

2. *Good Sense of Weight*

Many curlers with, or without, well-balanced swing deliveries have developed an uncanny sense of draw weight. Even those who use a sideways crouch in the hack have acquired, through practice, a sensitive finger-tip control, and can be counted on to create plenty of trouble for the so-called "style" player by executing a canny dead-weight draw or freeze shot at a time when his opponent is mentally scoring a big end for himself. Such curlers are legion. They are not too consistently "on the broom" with their side-arm or push deliveries, but their perfect tee-line-weight stones behind a convenient guard bring chuckles of enjoyment to the members of their own rink and under-the-breath mutterings of annoyance from the rival skip.

But here we are concerned with the player who has developed a clean delivery motion and whom we are watching to see if he has acquired this delicate sense of weight. He must not be the man who has two weights only: viz., draw weight and "bang-out" weight, but one who can differentiate between, and execute consistently, (a) Draw weight, (b) Front-ring weight, (c) Guard weight, (d) Back-ring weight, (e) Light-hack weight, (f) Hack weight, and (g) Heavy-hack weight. Of all these, draw, or tee-line, weight is the basis for obtaining the others. A player must feel sure of draw weight first; then, when during any game he has developed confidence in making that shot, it is a simple matter to increase or decrease his weight the desired number of feet to execute any shot asked for. Making the shot depends on getting the broom and the weight. If a hack-weight shot is called for and the player is ten feet over-weight on normal ice, he will be fortunate if his stone strikes any part of the rock he is called on to take out. You may ask, why does a skip have to be so fussy about indicating the weight desired by a matter of four feet or so when any weight within a range of twenty feet will strike some part of the offending stone that is to be removed. The answer is obvious. A good skip or curler not only wants the opposing rock removed but he wants his player's stone to roll to another point in the "house". That may be because he desires (1) a roll behind a guard, (2) a double take-out, (3) a roll in front of a "nest" of opposition stones, (4) to avoid bunching his own stones, or any of a score of other things. By playing the exact weight required for the ice given, the player is helping his rink to play for "position" and thereby to carry out the strategy of the skip.

There is no doubt, then, why a skip, when selecting his players, wants his men to have the feel of weight in all the shots they may be called upon to make. Too many curlers cannot resist an inner urge to hit a rock hard rather than pass it through quietly. Thereby they reduce their efficiency by fifty percent. They should control their impulses and play carefully for the wick or roll, thus making it more difficult for the opponent who has to play his shot next. A skip wants good offensive players on his team. A man who can draw and play quiet weight for position is an offensive player. The defensive curlers want to blast anything in sight. Keep that in mind next time you play. Learn to control your impulses and your weight.

3. *Practice*

Up to a few years ago it was possible, at least in the West, to find ice available at certain periods of the day for practice. To-day, with steadily increasing membership rosters, double-draws in the evenings and rented ice during the day, it is virtually impossible to find a spare sheet of ice for this purpose. Yet, where there is a will, there is a way, even if it means locking up the club after midnight in order to get an hour or so to perfect some flaw in delivery or to practise a certain type of shot that has been giving you trouble.

Practice can take many different forms:
1. Instructional periods
2. Individual play
3. Singles
4. Doubles
5. Substituting in a club game
6. Club games
7. Special matches
8. Out of town bonspiels

The first four methods of practice may be safely used to iron out individual problems involving slight changes in style where the player is experimenting with a new theory that calls for a change in stance, back swing, forward swing, or for a change in the position or movement of any part of the body during the mechanics of the swing. The last four methods noted should be utilized to perfect a style or particular change in position or motion by playing all normal shots asked for in a regular game so that the player will not be experimenting at the expense of his team.

a. Instructional Periods

Not to my knowledge has any curling club made provision for regularly scheduled instructional periods when drawing a programme of matches and events for the season. This is a glaring omission, and would be remedied immediately if programme committees had enough foresight to adopt a long-range attitude towards membership problems of future years. Dozens of curlers in every club would gladly attend and profit from such classes. As individuals, we cannot see our own mistakes no matter how we strive for perfection. It requires critical observation by someone else to detect flaws. Once the flaws are pointed out they can be eliminated either through our own knowledge of what to do or through the explanation and advice of another.

If such practice periods were provided for in the programme, five or six of the better curlers in the club would gladly offer their time for instruction and advice to "green" curlers, to new members, and, for that matter, to the older and more experienced players, too. A short meeting of instructors beforehand might be arranged to draw up a plan of instruction so that each period would be devoted to some particular problem. There follows a suggested outline of topics that might be used profitably during a course each year, providing for ten instructional periods per season. These periods need be only of one-half hour duration, the first ten minutes of which could be devoted to demonstration and instruction with the last twenty minutes for practice, observation, and constructive criticism.

PROGRAMME OF INSTRUCTION

1st NIGHT—(a) Preparing for delivery
       (b) The stance
       (c) The grip
2nd NIGHT—(a) The backswing

          1. *Position at start*
            — the handle
            — the feet
            — the arms
            — the hands
            — the shoulders and head

2. *Position at top of swing*
— the hands
— the arms
— the feet
— the shoulders and head
— the legs

3rd NIGHT—(a) The forward swing
1. *Movement of*
— the hands
— the feet
— the shoulders and head
— the arms
— the legs

4th NIGHT—(a) The follow-through
1. *Use of*
— the eyes
— the right arm and hand
— the left foot
— the left arm and broom
— the right leg and toe

5th NIGHT—(a) The full swing—along the line of direction
1. Starting position of stone
2. Checking line of delivery
3. Practise delivery—checking the line of delivery on follow-through
4. Counteracting—wide or narrow deliveries

6th NIGHT—(a) Turning the handle
1. Checking number of turns
2. Checking ice required for slow and fast turns
(b) Sweeping
1. How to hold the broom
2. Rhythmic motion of feet while sweeping
3. How to follow the stone

7th NIGHT—(a) Reading the ice
For the player (see Chapter 4).

8th to 10th
NIGHTS—Instructions to skips
Black board, chalk talks—(see Chapter 4)

The programme suggested above may be re-classified again by breaking up the groups during each instruction period into two, three, or more sections, as follows:

1. "Green" or first year curlers
    (a) Older curlers
    (b) Young curlers
2. Curlers of limited experience
    (a) Older
    (b) Younger
3. Experienced curlers
    (a) Older
    (b) Younger

b. INDIVIDUAL PLAY

Sometimes it is possible for an individual to locate a sheet of ice for practice. If such is the case for you, be careful not to fatigue your muscles by throwing too many stones. How long it is safe to practise will depend on your physical condition and on how early it is in the season. Once your muscles are tired or sore there is no value in further practice. It will do more harm than good.

Take no more than four stones for practice. Do not start throwing them up the ice indiscriminately. Exercise just as much preparation and care in delivering each one as you would in a regular game. Practise delivery and weight primarily during these sessions. Pick out a spot at the end of the rink as a substitute for the skip's broom and concentrate your undivided attention on that spot during the swing and follow-through.

PRACTICE SUGGESTIONS

Beginners, and those experimenting with changes in delivery, should practice:

1. Delivery for balance and rhythm
2. Delivery for line of direction
3. Delivery for weight

Players who want practice involving a good routine might try this:

1. Four shots—to limber up and get the feel of the ice and the weight required
2. Four draw shots—two in-turns and two out-turns
3. Two draws followed by two quiet take-outs
4. Two draws followed by two guards

5. Two draws to the side of the house followed by two "back ring weight" wick-ins

6. Finish up with four hack-weight take-outs by previously placing four other stones across the tee line at two foot intervals

A total of twenty-four stones thrown in any one practice session is more than sufficient for the average curler. Do not overdo it during practice for the muscles of your right arm and left leg may not feel sore at the time but they will the next day. Early in the season, twelve to twenty deliveries are sufficient. Later, as your endurance increases, a maximum of thirty stones delivered one after the other may be attempted. This applies to singles and doubles as a method of practice too. When you play doubles there is a greater time lapse between deliveries and you will find that throwing thirty stones will not be as hard on you as in individual practice.

If you would like something more interesting in practice sessions later on in the season, try Bob Dunbar's famous recipe. Dunbar was a noted "hitter" and his daily practice consisted of setting up five or six stones on the tee line at the far end of the ice, about a foot apart. Then he played until he could replace each one of those perfectly with six well-directed take-out shots. It will take the average curler many sessions to attain such mastery.

An excellent pastime for concentrating on the correct line of delivery and proper weight is the fascinating "draw-the-port" play. Set up two stones two-and-a-half feet apart on either side of the centre line and about six feet in front of the house. The object is to draw into the house without disturbing either stone in front. Score yourself as follows:

1. 4 points—if your stone gets through the port safely and stops within the eight-foot circle

2. 3 points—if it stops on or in the eight-foot or twelve-foot ring

3. 2 points—if you reach the rings but rub one of the guards

4. 1 point —if you negotiate the port but fail to remain on the rings

5. 0 points—if you do not reach the rings, or if you reach

the rings by passing by the outside of the
guard rocks

There are hundreds of other such innovations for practice. Use
your imagination and you will enjoy these sessions immensely.

c. SINGLES PRACTICE

If you like company, get another player. Deliver four stones
each and play from opposite ends of the sheet, each man holding
the broom for the other. Normally this is better than having both
players take turns throwing from the same hack, as it provides a
target (other player's broom) for delivery. Here are several interesting games for singles:

1. *Four stones a side game*

Play as you would in a regular game and keep score. Playing for the coffee or a suitable liquid substitute adds impetus
and develops more concentration.

2. *Points game*

Even if the ice has not been marked for the ten different
shots required for this game, any Curling Association programme
will illustrate the placement of the stones preparatory to playing
the various shots this exciting game demands

(a) Striking (b) Inwicking (c) Drawing (d) Guarding
(e) Chap and Lie (f) Wick and Curl in (g) Raising (h) Drawing
through a Port (i) Chipping the Winner (j) Outwick.

Four stones are played for each type of shot stipulated. A
perfect score is 72 (maximum two points per stone). To my
knowledge the highest score ever recorded in an officially recognized game was 52, so it can be readily understood why the points
game is a real test of skill.

3. *Charity-draw game*

During World War II the Charity-Draw originated when
Manitoba curlers were raising money for overseas parcels for
the Red Cross.

Each player was required to pay five cents per stone attempted.
The shot required in every case was a simple draw. If the
player's stone touched the eight-foot circle his five cents was

returned. If it was inside the eight-foot circle he collected a dime; fifteen cents if it touched the four-foot circle; twenty cents if the stone rested on the two-foot circle, and if he managed to cover the button or the one foot circle, his reward was a quarter. Needless to say the Red Cross did well financially. Any two players may play this game and each take turns at being banker if pecuniary interest is found necessary. A few weeks at this game in your spare time will gain any player sizeable respect for his draw game.

4. *Wick and Roll*

The wick and roll shot demands real accuracy in delivery and perfect weight control. It calls for wicking in off a stone placed on the twelve-foot or eight-foot circle in the 1 o'clock or 2 o'clock area, to a position on the other side of the centre line and directly behind a guard which has been placed in front of the rings. The stone off which the wick is to be made may be changed in position frequently to call for thinner or thicker wicks. Points may be scored according to the degree of the roll-in after the wick, a maximum of four points being given if the player's stone is more than half buried behind the guard.

d. DOUBLES PRACTICE

Four players pair off to equalize curling ability on either side. Eight stones a side are normally used. Two opposing players act as skips at each end, thus no moving of players from one end to the other is required. The rotation of delivery is the same as that followed in a regular match game and the scoring is identical.

This type of practice gives each player a chance to "read" the ice for his partner as well as experience in skipping strategy, judging weight of approaching stones and measuring the ice required for each shot. It is possible to practise over a longer period but no more stones would be delivered by each player because of the waiting period while the partner and his opponent are delivering from the other end of the ice. The doubles game is more advisable for practice earlier in the season until the muscles are tuned up.

e. Substituting in a Club Game

Playing in a regularly scheduled match does not allow for much experimentation. It is hardly fair to the team for whom you are playing to try to correct your bad habits at their expense. Concentrate on your follow-through and weight. You obtain very little practice in such a game, for much of your energy will be expended in meeting the demands of your skip in sweeping. In a ten-end game you will deliver twenty stones which would take just twenty minutes in a practice session. If a player wants to condition himself for a bonspiel there is no better way, but if I had my choice I would prefer any of the other methods of practice referred to in this chapter.

f. Club Games and Special Matches

In playing in club games and other matches, as an aid in practice, it must be kept in mind that pure practice sessions are for the express purpose of ironing out "kinks" in the delivery and practising any particular type of shot that has been giving trouble. Such play also develops and smooths out the rhythm of the swing as well as the feel of weight. On the other hand, club games aid the player in learning to curl well under the pressure of real competition. In such games the player is practising:

1. Concentration
2. Competitiveness—ability to make his shots under pressure
3. Consistency—steadiness and dependability.
4. Building up self-confidence
5. Judging weight of a stone while sweeping or following it
6. Judging of ice under all types of conditions

These are the finer points and require the player to be constantly exposed to the necessity of curling under such competitive conditions. The experience gained in all curling games gradually builds up a vast store of knowledge and confidence that makes the difference between a good curler and a seasoned, tried, and proven campaigner.

g. Out of Town Bonspiels

To put the finishing touches to practice sessions and to participation in club games and other matches, go to an outside bonspiel where opponents, ice condiitons, and stones present vastly different problems. Bonspiel play requires taking part in six to ten games in a relatively short period. It will tone up your muscles, put balance into your delivery swing, and give you plenty of practice playing every shot in your repertoire. By the time you have played the last stone and made tracks for home you should have a fine edge on your game. If you are not then ready for the major competitions, you never will be.

If any curler is willing to follow religiously the procedures for practice I have outlined above for at least a few years, he will reach a degree of skill that will astound him. I have often heard it said that if a curler would adhere as rigidly to practice and play as many ardent golfers do, he could achieve a proficiency of spectacular proportions. To-day it is not uncommon for a curling team to make 65% of its shots in an important match and still win the game. There is no reason why the average percentage shouldn't be closer to 80% on normal ice if the individual players would spend the necessary time in practice and play.

4. Sweeping

Through the centuries the besom and stane (broom and rock) have been inseparable symbols of the game of curling. At bonspiel time a curler is always identifiable by the broom he carries or the tam he wears. The broom, particularly, is his trade-mark and his indispensable ally on the ice, for not only does it serve him in the normal pursuit of his pastime but in waving a greeting to a friend, playfully nudging someone's ribs, defending his shins from ricocheting stones, signalling scores, pushing rocks off the ice, supporting the weight of a tired body, scratching an itchy spot, and keeping the trousers clean when used as a seat. The trusty old broom is an asset of incalculable value.

There are those who would remove the broom from the curler's kit, or, at least, when they argue that sweeping has no effect on the movement of a stone, they are indirectly suggesting that the broom may as well be stacked permanently in the basement. Yet these locker-room lawyers would be the first to refuse to sign membership cards if, when a new season rolled around, they were informed that henceforth brooms and sweeping were to be divorced from curling. Why? For many reasons. Let me enumerate a few and, in so doing, separate broom and sweeping in the analysis:

HAS SWEEPING ANY VALUE IN CURLING?

The chief arguments centre around the physical values of sweeping. Does sweeping help a stone to travel further? Does sweeping help a rock to get past a guard or prevent it from curling too much? Several scientific experiments have been performed to settle this needless controversy. In some cases the reports stated no physical benefits; in others, word arrived that the effects were considerable. Whom are we to believe? Such experiments to me would be inconclusive unless tests were:

1. Performed under all ice conditions
2. Performed with powerful sweepers who knew how and where to sweep, and who were co-ordinated sweepers
3. Performed with sufficient pairs of matched stones with varied running surfaces to analyze results of sweeping on new stones and older stones

Personally, I am convinced, as a result of participation in thousands of games under all conditions, that sweeping helps the distance a stone travels more than it helps its direction, but only in proportion to (1) the power and effectiveness of the sweepers, (2) the keenness of the ice surface, (3) the smoothness of the running surface of the stones. Naturally, the greatest help is given during the last few feet of the stone's course. To my mind, here are the chief reasons why the opponents of sweeping can lay claim to justifying their arguments:

SWEEPING AIDS A STONE LITTLE OR NONE

When — 1. A sweeper uses long, light strokes
2. A stone is travelling fast
3. The ice is frosty or wet
4. A sweeper sweeps too far in front of the stone
5. A fast but light sweeping stroke is used
6. A take-out or running shot is played

    7. A broom with too loose, too long, or too short straw
       is used

But if our doubting brothers want to see a draw-weight stone move five or six feet farther (I am inclined to discredit claims of twelve to fifteen feet, except on downhill ice) let me watch two men on reasonably keen ice sweep:

    1. Next to the stone with strokes synchronized

    2. Immediately in the path of the stone

    3. With short, fast and powerful strokes that literally
       pound the ice

    4. The last thirty feet of the stone's course and continu-
       ing to sweep until the stone has come to a dead stop

Too many curlers put all their energy into sweeping during the early stages and have little power left in their strokes when the stone is dying—the time when sweeping is doing the most good. They should keep leaning on that broom until the rock stops completely, and not quit when the stone has only a foot or two to go.

There seems no earthly doubt that powerful sweeping does tend to create a vacuum in front of the stone and also because ice is not resistant like glass, the friction effected by fast, strong sweepers not only polishes the ice surface but lessens the resistance of the ice to the cup of the stone in much the same way as the ice crystals yield under the pressure of skates.

Now for argument's sake, let us agree with the critics that ordinary sweeping does not materially affect the course of a stone. Give them the benefit of any doubt, for the moment, and wait until one of these misguided friends gets into a nip-and-tuck battle for the Group "D" championship. The score is tied "coming home". His skip asks for a draw to the eight-foot circle. He delivers and his weight appears good, but just as it crosses the "hog" line he thinks his stone is going to be short. Why does he suddenly start to bellow, "Sweep! Sweep!" at the top of his lungs? No, he does not believe that sweeping is of any use and he may honestly feel that way—after the game is over. But on the impulse of the moment, and under stress of high nervous tension, both he and the sweepers respond instantly to the urge to help that stone into the "house" if they can, whether it is done through the medium of physical labour or ear-splitting yells of encouragement. Yes, our friend will have to agree on that point. He will also have to agree that sweeping keeps a player on his toes and keyed up to competitive tension. Have you ever seen a highly-competitive player who is not alive in his body as well as his mind? As a skip, I'll take the man who goes at the game with real zest, and as a sweeper poises himself over every rock ready to stroke with his broom at the slightest urging. Take sweeping out of curling and you take all the colour and excitement out of the game. The familiar roars of the skip will die away to whispers; the tenseness and alacrity of the players will melt to mild indifference, and the buzz from excited spectators "behind the glass" will be replaced by the snores of the caretaker.

The art of sweeping is sadly neglected by many curlers or, should I say, most beginners are never taught how to sweep properly. Is it so simple to acquire the three things every good sweeper requires: (1) Power, (2) Co-ordination, (3) Rhythm? A careful study of the simple mechanics and a little practice in the back shed will produce amazing results.

HOLDING THE BROOM

A right-hander usually places his left hand down the shaft and his right at the top of the handle (see Fig. 54). The reverse holds true in the case of a southpaw. If you are a right-hander, place the left hand in a palm-up position as far down the shaft as is necessary to give you the proper leverage. This will depend on your height and the strength of your wrists. The thumb of the left hand is placed on the shaft and pointing downward. The right hand grasps the top of the handle (see Fig. 55) and the thumb or forefinger (usually the forefinger) presses on top of the shaft. The function of the right hand is to transmit the muscular pressure of the body, shoulders, and arm in giving the broom stroke power or the feeling of "leaning on the broom" during the sweeping motion. The left hand and wrist give flexibility and speed, as well as extra power, to the stroke (see Fig. 56).

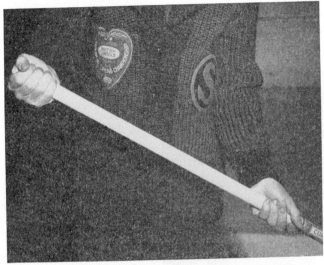

Fig. 54 — POSITION OF THE HANDS ON A BROOM

A player who sweeps on the left hand side of a stone normally grips the handle of the broom as shown above. Some players reverse the position of the left hand with the thumb pointing up the shaft. Normally a more powerful sweeping stroke is obtained by using the grip shown.

Fig. 55

GRIP OF THE RIGHT HAND ON THE BROOM SHAFT

Notice the position of the thumb pressing the top of the handle. This pressure is necessary to transmit power to the stroke while the left hand acts as the lever to move the broom back and forward. The right hand acts as a fulcrum during the sweeping motion and exerts a downward pressure at the same time.

FOOT-WORK IN SWEEPING

Rhythm in sweeping is achieved by co-ordinating the motion of the feet with that of the wrists and arms. The first thing to learn is to sweep while in a stationary position, that is to sweep without attempting to move up the ice. Take up your position holding the broom as illustrated. Without attempting to move your broom, mark time with your feet: left—right; left—right; left—right. That gives you the natural motion of the feet while sweeping. Now start

Fig. 56

SWEEPING POWER

Sweeping power is illustrated by Ness Wise. His left hand and wrist provide flexibility and the right hand exerts the downward pressure to give power to the stroke. Note the left hand on top of the broom shaft, position of the feet, and the slight turn of the body to the left.

Fig. 57 — A GOOD SWEEPING COMBINATION

Both players are sweeping close to the stone and directly across its path. Note the right hand of the sweeper on the left is placed under the broom shaft. The side-stepping motion of the feet is clearly visible here.

moving your broom forward and back across the ice (imagine that you are sweeping in front of a stationary stone) once forward and back with each step. Thus—left (forward and back); right (forward and back), and so on. Crouch a little so that your broom straw rests on the ice. Repeat the performance, left (forward and back), right (forward and back). Bend your knees a little; get up a bit more on the balls of your feet; stroke a little faster and break into a standstill trot—left—right; left—right; faster, faster; speed up the stroke of your broom to keep pace. Try this every day on the cellar floor or in the back wood-shed until the rhythm comes naturally. Once you feel natural pounding the floor in this stationary position, try moving along the ice (or floor) with the same rhythm and keep speeding up your movement until you are able to trot or even to run and sweep without disturbing that left (forward and back), right (forward and back) rhythm.

The left-right rhythm when the sweeper is moving along with a stone can be developed to fit any speed of motion required. However, the feet use a side-stepping motion in following the stone (see Fig. 57), and the body is turned forward about twenty degrees. A right-hander (i.e. one who sweeps with the left hand down the shaft) should keep to the left side of a stone when sweeping. The left foot, during the sweeping motion of a good sweeper who sweeps close to the stone, will seldom be ahead of the rock (see Fig. 58).

POSITION OF THE BODY AND HEAD

As previously mentioned, a good sweeper will always be partly turned forward so that he can readily take a quick glance to see what is ahead and therefore judge the weight of the stone more accurately. The head at all times is kept fairly well down in order to get the utmost pressure on the broom but not so far that occasional glances can't be taken to size up the course and speed of the stone (see Fig. 57).

SELECTION AND CARE OF A BROOM

Notwithstanding the trend in some sections of the country towards placing of brooms on each sheet for curlers' use, I still favour the opinion that complete standardization of brooms is not an aid to better curling. Even though the type of broom selected for common

Fig. 58 — SYNCHRONIZED MOTION

Note that the right hand player who is sweeping next to the stone has his body well back of the stone. His left foot moves up alongside the stone at this point, but seldom ahead of it. Notice the synchronized motion of the brooms.

use is satisfactory according to general specifications, it will not satisfy all the requirements of any one individual. For me a broom is personalized and becomes an integral part after it is "broken-in". The weight of the broom, the length of the handle, the length of the straw, the binding of the straw, and the balance of weight between the handle and the straw give me a sense of security that cannot be found in a strange broom. In addition, every curler uses a broom differently in sweeping, and the bias that he uses wears the straw unevenly. For another curler the "feel" of the broom is lost. Perhaps I am too sensitive about such things, but anytime I have a strange broom in my hand, I am conscious of it, particularly during the delivery when I should be free to concentrate solely on a rhythmic swing.

The broom selected will depend on the stature and build of the individual. The physically robust curler will want a heavier broom with heavy straw; a slightly built player will prefer a light-weight broom with lighter straw.

Most curling brooms have standard length handles, but it takes a tall, well-built man to get a short fast stroke with such a handle. For years, all members of my rink have made it a practice to saw three to four inches off the top of the handle. As a result, we get much better leverage, and a faster stroke is possible. The shorter the player, the shorter his broom handle should be.

Another fetish of mine is to use a pair of scissors to cut an inch or two off the long straw of a new broom so as to get even length in the straw. This practice not only gives the broom a well-groomed appearance but, by shortening the length of the straw, a shorter and faster sweeping motion can be attained. In addition, after trimming the straw I take a length of heavy string or cord and weave it through the straw an inch or so below the last row of factory binding, for the following reasons: (1) to prevent straws breaking off at the normal binding (which is very tight), thus lengthening the life of the broom; (2) to pull the long straw together so that, during the pressure of the broom on the ice while sweeping, the straw does not spread so much and thus lose power in the stroke (see Fig. 59). By this extra binding, which is flexible yet strengthening to the long straw, the sweeper can almost beat the ice in his stroke. When a powerful sweeper uses such a broom, you can hear it pounding the ice like a rug beater.

Fig. 59

Extra Binding

An extra binding of ordinary cord woven above the factory binding not only lengthens the life of a broom, but adds more power to the sweeping stroke as well.

If proper care is taken of your broom, it should last for one season. Some strong sweepers who play in sixty or more games a year will require two brooms, but the extra binding described above will add 50% to the life of a broom and you will get more power out of it as well. Be careful in selecting a broom to choose one with an evenly grained handle. A flaw in the grain has caused many a broken handle. When placing the broom in the locker, stand it on its handle, otherwise the straw will bend and warp, making it difficult to sweep with as well as adding to the hazard of loose straws on the ice. There should be a law against a player who is careless about looking after his broom. He is public enemy number one on the ice. Loose straws from his broom fly with abandon and many a good shot is irretrievably lost through his unforgiveable carelessness. Seldom does he pay in mental anguish for his own criminal negligence. It is always the other fellow.

Qualities of a Good Sweeper

It is rare indeed to find a curler who possesses all the qualities demanded of a good sweeper. So far I have mentioned only the sweeping qualities, but there are several other compensating features which are worth mention. For completeness, I will list them all first.

1. Power
2. Rhythm
3. Sense of direction
4. Sense of weight
5. Knowing when to sweep
6. Poise and alertness
7. Proper mental attitude

Power and rhythm have been dealt with fully. A clever sweeper will note the position of the skip's broom while waiting for his team-mate to deliver, then as the stone is released he can tell from its position relative to the centre line whether it is on the broom or wide or narrow. Then he will act accordingly. If you have ever watched high-calibre rinks in action, you will notice few signals and little bellowing from the skip. His well-trained sweepers act almost instinctively.

When it comes to developing a keen sense of weight, you will have to hunt far and wide to find such a sweeper. At this point, I would like to pay a compliment to my original second man, Marvin Macintyre, who played with me from 1928 to 1939. Little Mac, as we called him, was uncanny in his sense of weight in sweeping a stone. He could literally take it to a dime on the ice. He knew to a few inches how far it would travel, and he acted accordingly every time. I developed such confidence in his amazing ability that before I stepped into the hack I always told Mac where I was trying to place the rock. Time and time again Mac made me look "awfully" good on my draw shots. He seemed to coax the stone through sweeping, or alert watching, right to the exact spot. Not an inch too far or too short did he take it. He was a powerful sweeper, too, and a real competitor. This sense of weight is almost a sixth sense, and is developed only after many years of experience, and then by only a few curlers.

Often a sweeper is beset on one side by the skip hollering at him to sweep and on the other by the player who has delivered the stone yelling, "Whoa!" What a dilemma! Whom is he to listen to? I must honestly confess that I have been guilty in many cases where I have followed my stone up the ice yelling "Yes! Yes!" one second, and "Wait! Wait" the next. All the while, brother Grant, the third, who is standing at the "head" is wailing at the sweepers to do just the opposite. Sweepers all over the world suffer moments like these, and many have growled to themselves: "Why in h — — don't they make up their minds?"

Who, then, the man on the "head" or the player following the stone, is in the better position to judge weight? The answer is "neither", if the sweepers know their jobs, but, as I mentioned previously, few sweepers have the experience or the confidence, therefore the man on the "head" should be in the better position if a decision has to be made. It is easier to judge the weight of a stone coming towards you than one going away from you. Sometimes the player following the stone is in a better position to judge the direction of the rock, but not the weight. Knowing when to sweep is a matter of knowing exactly where the rock is supposed to go, and why.

Sweepers should watch carefully all the signals given by the skip so that, if a guard is required, they know whether it is a short or long guard; whether it is preferable to guard against an in-turn or an out-turn take-out; whether it should be swept past another guard or allowed to stop short. These are all important problems in a close match, and the sweepers require to be as mentally alert as the skip. Curling is a team game, and the exact positional play of each stone is a relative part of the over-all strategy. Sweeping plays a very important part in it.

One obvious error committed by most sweepers is, that, after following the stone down the ice, they suddenly decide their work is

Fig. 60

WATCHFUL SWEEPER

Marv. Macintyre depicts the alert sweeper poised and ready for sweeping action. Note the side-stepping motion of the feet; a partly-turned body and the eyes of the sweeper attentive to the speed of the stone.

done before the rock is dead (usually in the last three or four feet, in the case of a draw or guard). An alert sweeper will follow the stone and remain crouched over it, poised and ready to use his broom, even during the last few inches of the course of a stone (see Fig. 60). The extra curl of half an inch sometimes provides a formidable barrier for an opponent's rock, or an inch or two further will bury the rock completely behind a guard or "freeze" it to an opposing stone, or move it back far enough to spoil the chances of your opposition playing a double wick. Keep on the job to the last second. Games are won and lost on such precisional care.

Far and away the greatest of all qualities in a sweeper is the moral and mental uplift given to the other members of his rink by a favourable attitude towards the importance of sweeping. Nothing breaks the heart and courage of a team mate sooner than a half-hearted attempt by the sweepers of his rink. He is immediately prone to think that his efforts are being slighted. And nothing is finer for team morale than to have your sweepers "get in there and pitch" to make your shot look good. I guess I do sound like a skip, don't I, but whether you are the lowly lead, or the skip's "mate", the important thing for you in a game is the right mental attitude, and good sweeping will do more than enough to bolster your self-confidence. Do your share to help your team mates develop the same indomitable outlook. You will make a good team man if you learn how to sweep effectively and well, because you will give your men the feeling of inner satisfaction that comes from a well-swept stone, and with it the self-confidence that will make them better curlers. More mutual help from the sweepers will cause less "bile secretion" among curlers, and eliminate the swallowing of many bitter pills of dissatisfaction.

Synchronization of Good Sweepers

Only once had I the pleasure of having a left- and a right-hand sweeper as lead and second on my rink. Both were powerful sweepers who could synchronize their broom strokes so that they swept one broom width in front of the stone in motion. Their rhythmic pounding of the ice was a thing of beauty to watch. Perfect footwork as they glided along the ice on either side of the rock made their hard sweeping appear effortless—a real symmetry of motion. Sad to relate, neither of these men kept on with their curling. Ted Linklater and "Shiner" Chambers were their names. I hope my "short" draw shots had nothing to do with their absence from the game to-day.

In most cases you will have two right handers sweeping on the same side of the stone. This has been my own experience for the past twenty years. One of these men will of necessity have to sweep next to the stone and it should be the one who is the more powerful sweeper and if possible the one who sweeps with his broom well ahead of his body. If this combination can be found, the second broom will not be sweeping too far ahead of the first. The closer they are, the better. Care must be taken to see that both sweepers use the same line of direction in their strokes of the broom or frequent clashes may cause a broom to strike the rock that is being swept. A deflected stone is automatically removed from play and may be very costly. If the more powerful sweeper is next to the stone his broom will not be affected too often by clashing with the broom of the weaker sweeper.

Conserving Energy in Sweeping

In bonspiel play where one game follows on the heels of another, too much sweeping is injurious to effective curling, particularly in the case of a curler who is not physically able to stand up under it. In the case of the members of my own rink, none of us is built along the lines of the mythical Paul Bunyan, so it is vitally necessary that we conserve our energy and make certain that when we get into the hack our muscles are not completely fatigued. If the muscles are numb through heavy exertion you will lose the "feel" of the stone during delivery. They must be given a chance to regain their resiliency before delivery. That is why, after the lead and second have swept hard on my last stone, I wait two or even three minutes so that the lead man can regain the feel of his muscles before giving him the ice for his first shot in the following end. Sweeping is of vital importance in curling but it is secondary to the playing of the stones. It is not of much value, then, for a man to do so well with his sweeping that he is utterly useless in the hack.

There are several ways of conserving energy yet maintaining the morale that good sweeping gives to any team.

1. Players alternate in sweeping lead and second stones with the second sweeping the first of the lead's stones so he will be rested when his turn comes to play. Similarly the third sweeps the first of the second's stones.
2. The skip may "come out" to meet a stone and follow it or sweep it into position, thus relieving his sweepers. This is advisable only in the case of open draw shots.
3. Relax and sit down between shots when the game is well in hand, but keep your eye on every stone that is thrown.

4. Coast during the first stages of sweeping a stone then "bear down" during the last few feet.

5. Sweep in relays for the lead and second rocks. One sweeper "takes" the stone to the second "hog" line and the second sweeper from there in.

6. If the game is well in hand, the skip should have his players use a little firmer weight to play for rolls in the case of take-outs. Less sweeping is required for these shots.

7. The skip can aid the sweeper to conserve energy by giving sufficient ice for a take-out shot. Many skips are guilty of "pinching" the ice for their players. This necessitates more sweeping than would be necessary if the full complement of ice were given in the first place. Actually more shots are missed through taking narrow ice than by being wide of the broom.

Judgment of Ice and Weight

Many curlers seem to adopt the attitude that the skip is the only one on the rink who is supposed to do any thinking, apart from the third, or vice-skip, who occasionally steps into the picture with a word or two. There may be some merit in the ancient theory that the skip does most of the talking, but heaven help the team where he does all the thinking! A perfect rink is made up of four individuals who are in complete thinking harmony with each other. That is, when a skip calls for a certain shot and "gives ice" for that shot, all other three members mentally agree that the ice given and the weight called for is correct. But the other three have to know the ice as well as the skip does if they are to agree. An indifferent acquiescence to the skip's instructions is of no value whether the player has subscribed to the creed "I trust in my skipper" or not. If the player is keen and competitive, he will feel satisfied in his own mind from previous observation he has made that he can make the shot asked for by using the ice and weight suggested by his skip.

In order to achieve this beatific frame of mind a player must be attentive to, and observant of, what is going on around him, so that a blueprint of the sheet of ice he is playing on is gradually taking shape in his mind, as well as a quick analysis of the keenness or heaviness of the ice surface.

JUDGING WEIGHT

Have you ever run across a "lead" who could consistently draw to the "house" with the first stone he delivered in any one game? Not likely you have. During my experience I have come into contact with two "lead" men who were surprisingly good at sensing weight during the first end. Both of these men were particularly observant, and one of them was, by nature, given to experiment as well. Both took a look at the temperature in the rink before the game started; examined the pebble on the ice to see whether it was fine or coarse; watched the progress of the first stone delivered on the adjoining sheet; examined the cups of the stones they were to play with (if they were strange stones). The lead, with experimental bent, nudged a stone with his toe several times before the game started to see how quickly it stopped after sliding a few feet. These observations and experiments gave both a pretty fair clue to the keenness of the ice surface on that particular sheet, and they were never very far out in playing that first draw shot. Once the player has the feel of draw weight (tee-line weight), he can measure easily the weight required for most other shots.

JUDGING ICE

A player is much more handicapped than the skip in judging the "pull" or curl of a rock during the first few ends of a game because he seldom has the opportunity of standing directly in line with the shot, but at each end, when he delivers his own pair of stones, he has a chance to "size up" the ice. When his opponents and team mates are delivering, he still must keep his eye on the ice, and if it is a tricky sheet, special concentration is needed. Therefore, when his turn comes to get into the hack, he should have a pretty accurate idea of what his rock will do, with the ice given and the weight required. Many times the skip is hazy about what weight is to be used, then the enterprising curler, having full knowledge of the ice, delivers with complete confidence. Just one bad miss early in a game through lack of attention to the ice will undermine any player's confidence in himself or the skip, and once this is lost or faltering, he will most likely play a bad game from then on.

WEARING APPAREL

Air temperature, blood circulation, and other factors influence the type and amount of clothing worn on the ice, yet wearing apparel can be vitally important in helping or hindering good curling. Since curlers are as superstitious as other men, many a player has refused to change his socks as long as his team was winning in bonspiel play; others have extended this fear to include long underwear. Shirts, gloves, ties, hats, and even handkerchief, were never allowed to enter the laundry bag or the cleaners until the magic spell had worn off. Yet there is valid, if unconscionable, reason for all this fuss. In a certain pair of socks, or a particular shirt, the player feels comfortable. Sometimes, unknown to him, an old shirt is roomier and allows more freedom of motion. Never will I forget one lamentable year when for some reason unbeknown to me, I lost my draw weight touch which had always been my specialty. That year in bonspiel time, I changed my socks and shirts and ties regularly, trying to find the winning combination, but the spell never lasted more than a few games. Then another change of shirt or socks, and still the draw weight refused to show up. After the bonspiel was over I suddenly found the cause. I had been changing everything but my shoes. They were the guilty offenders. No kidding! I had purchased a pair of heavier brogues that fall before curling started, and I had been using these brogues all winter. Every year previous I had worn thin-soled shoes which allowed me to slide on the toe of the foot. The brogues were too thick to allow me to get up on the toe of the foot while sliding, and not realizing the change in type of shoe, I had been riding the flat of the foot all winter, and with it lost the fine touch of weight.

Comfortable, flexible, roomy clothing is most important in allowing complete freedom of movement. Any clothing that binds the shoulders or arms is bound to affect the delivery. As a player, you want a free and unrestricted swing, unencumbered by tight or heavy clothing.

Shoes and gloves require the greatest care in selection. They should be snug but not tight. They should not be too heavy for the hands and feet should almost feel "through". Shoes give you your footing and balance. Gloves give you the "feel" of the stone. Select both painstakingly.

A few years ago the club mates of a team that had just won the right to represent Manitoba in the Canadian Finals were so proud that they collected enough money to purchase a complete new outfit for the winning rink. They were equipped from head to toe. Hats, shirts, ties, sweaters, trousers, socks, shoes, all matched to present a very smart appearance, but somehow I think the newness of their smart gear contributed more than a little to very mediocre play in the finals.

Previous Experience and Positions Played

In selecting a good lead for a rink, a skip would be unwise to search among the seconds, thirds, and skips for his material. Just as four skips never make a good combination on a rink, similarly three seconds and a skip would seldom be effective. If you want a good lead man, select a player who has played that position for some time and whose specialty is the draw. The same applies in the case of other positions. Any skip should realize this, yet it is a common practice at the beginning of the season for him to select a rink composed of thirds and skips. On paper, the rink appears to have power, but in actual practice it seldom works out that way.

About fifteen years ago I had the good fortune to skip a rink to the Club Championship at the Strathcona Club in Winnipeg. Against the sternest competition in the Club, we lost but one game out of fourteen. This earned us the right to represent our club in the Provincial Brier Playdowns. When our lead man suggested that he might not be able to take part in the playoff, we decided that we had better take advantage of this and strengthen the team. So we secured the vice-skip of another strong rink, moved him in to second spot and dropped our regular second to the lead position. The results were astounding. Our reconverted lead who had played second all year never did catch draw weight and our imported second was lost playing in that position. We were fortunate to reach the semi-finals of one competition. If we had kept the original set-up intact we would have been curling like a well-oiled machine as we had done in our club games.

In my experience, a skip will sometimes make a good lead, but seldom a second or third man. I would rather choose an up-and-coming young man as a lead than an experienced second, third, or skip.

Once a player has curled in one position for a few years, he gains the perspective of that position. It will take him years to get the same perspective in another position. Candidly, after being a skip for thirty years, I would make a very poor second or third for any other skip because I have grown accustomed to sizing up my shot from the "head" not from the side ice or the hack.

Mental and Spiritual Characteristics

If I have deferred the mental and spiritual qualities required in a curler to the last, it is not because I consider them less important. In fact no man or woman will ever reach any heights in curling achievement without them. You have only to think back over the names of those you have curled with or against to find many individual cases where there was ever evidence of curling ability but somehow the spark was lacking that could kindle the flame of greatness. If any of us possess these abstract qualities, we need not become unduly conceited. Rather we can thank God for our heritage, environment, and in some cases our childhood upbringing.

I call these qualifications the Seven C's for Curling Success. Yet if you examine them closely you will find they may be applied to gain success in almost any line of endeavour. Frequently when asked to address groups of High School students I use the Seven C's as the basis of my talk.

Seven C's for Curling Success—

1. *Compatability*

When casting about for another player for a team, the questions that cross the mind are: "Will he fit in with the rest of the rink in a friendly, personal way?" "Have we much in common with him besides curling?" This may sound snobbish but snobbishness is not implied. Social and economic distinctions are often associated with curling in certain areas or curling clubs, but it should not apply to the most democratic of all games. There is no denying, though, that if four men have much in common through proximity of age, membership in allied trades or professions, and similar interests in outside organizations, that they will harmonize more completely than in cases where there is no common relationship off the ice. Of course, this companionship twelve months of the year can reach the point where the players know each other's idiosyncrasies too well, and too much familiarity often breeds contempt. But, generally, a bond stronger than that engendered by curling together two nights a week helps to strengthen the teamwork of a rink.

Age difference presents a hurdle. That is why, when young men out of school come to me about joining a senior curling club, I always tell them to get four fellows of their own age group together and form a rink. They will enjoy curling, and they will enjoy each other's company on and off the ice. Quite often, in off-the-ice sessions, a rink thrashes out problems in strategy and faults in delivery or thinking that would be missed entirely without these post-mortems. Curling is a sociable game and lends itself perfectly to fraternization before, during, and after the game. Why not select your team with this in mind, too?

2. Concentration

One New Year's afternoon at the Granite Club in Winnipeg, the finals of the Manitoba High School Boys' Bonspiel was in progress. Along about the eighth end the ice began to get "swingy". The temperature in the rink had been rising as a result of the large crowd witnessing the game and on each end, from the eighth end on, the rocks were "pulling" a little more. One of the school boy skips was so busy talking to well-wishers behind him that he neglected to watch his opponents' stones being played and failed to realize what was happening to the ice. When his turn came to play, he took a normal amount of ice for a draw shot and wondered why he raised his opponent in for shot. He did this not once but three times during the next three ends. Yes, through his carelessness and lack of concentration, he lost a game he should have won.

Concentration and attentiveness to every shot by every player are necessary. That is one thing I have to be thankful for in the case of my own rink. Harold Nelson of Carberry, Manitoba, once paid my boys a compliment I shall not soon forget. He made this remark during a game in the Brier Playdown, "Gosh, Ken, I wish my men would quit watching the game on the next sheet and take a look at our game. Your men are so busy watching every shot my men make, I'll bet they don't even know who is winning on the next sheet." With that he asked Lyal Dyker, our second: "Who is winning on Sheet 4?" Lyal had to turn and look at the scoreboard before answering.

Howard Wood is a great skip and a great competitor. When you are standing next to him on the ice, you almost feel a vibration caused by the intensity of his concentration. This habit is not reserved exclusively for skips. Other players should cultivate it, too.

3. Co-operation

There are a good many individualists in the world, and many of them find their way into the ranks of the curlers. Curling is a team game and has no room for the volatile egotist or the stubborn, untractable player who thinks the game revolves around him. This not only applies to skips, who are often branded with such a label, but to others as well. Team work requires the spirit of give and take, consideration of the other fellow, and a willingness to submerge impulsive individual desires in the common interest of the rink. There is little need here to cite examples, as this unsociable disease afflicts all of us at some time or another to a lesser or greater degree. Co-operation means confidence in the knowledge that your team mate or skip is doing his level best and that the other players think likewise of you. If you haven't confidence in your team mates, you shouldn't be playing with them. Too often curlers may have more confidence in their own judgment and ability than anyone else has. These individuals who are always right had better play "singles" where they have no one but themselves to blame if they miss a shot. Such curlers change from one rink to another every year or from one club to another, or failing that, they mercifully turn their individualism in the direction of another pastime.

It is the crabs, the grousers, the egocentrics who blame everyone and everything but themselves when things go wrong, that take the joy out of curling. Fortunately, I have never been exposed to such individuals for more than an hour or two in a curling game, but I am afraid that anyone tainted the least bit by that malady would not be selected on an all-star curling team.

4. Courage

as the "never-say-die" attitude or again as intestinal fortitude. At

Courage is a difficult quality to define. It has been referred to

any rate it is a spiritual or mental quality that few are fortunate

enough to possess. Sometimes I call it optimism, for a curler who is unwaveringly confident that while there is life there is hope will never suffer too much from an inferiority complex. It is not a physical courage but a healthy mental attitude that refuses to admit defeat even in the face of hopeless situations (and many such arise during a curler's experience).

I know of many curlers who have developed the mechanics of the game to perfection. They can make a "take-out and roll" perfectly; they can draw to a dime; they have a wide knowledge of skipping strategy, but a five end scored by the opposition causes them to fold up completely. As long as they are winning they can't be beaten, but as soon as their team is on the short end of the score, their chins drop and they pretend to be more interested in the game on the next sheet.

We all love a man who can come from behind, or who can get up off the floor and come back for more. This elusive quality is hard to determine in a curler, but if you see any sign of it and he has many of the other qualifications, sign him up. You will never regret it.

5. Confidence

There is not too clear a line between courage and confidence. Confidence is more of a mental attitude of self-reliance that exists in a player when he sits in the hack ready to play his shot. It is the feeling that the shot he is about to try is as good as made, irrespective of how difficult or how serious the situation is. Confidence is not conceit or braggadocio (which usually covers up lack of confidence) but a quiet inner conviction that the shot that you are about to try can be made and that you can and will make it. Never for one moment does the thought occur that you may not make it, nor is the mind troubled by fear of the consequence of what might happen if the shot is not made. Just as soon as doubt enters the mind, self-confidence beats a hasty retreat.

Once after playing a draw through a narrow port to the two foot circle to tie the score on the tenth end, the opposing skip said to me: "My God, Ken! You didn't expect to make that shot did you?" I replied sincerely and honestly when I said: "The thought never entered my mind that I might not make it." I was not bragging. It was true. It is an unexplainable frame of mind that I get every now and again. Naturally I don't feel this way all the time, but often under stress of competition that is exactly how my mind functions. Two or three bad misses will shake a player's confidence but it should bounce back quickly after he makes a shot or two. Part of the game is to get the opponents to miss so as to upset their self-confidence—but more about that in a later chapter.

Confidence comes through knowledge; knowledge of what the ice will do and what weight is required to make the shot. It also comes from a grooved delivery which is right on a line with the broom. Develop a good delivery, know your weight, watch the ice carefully and you will quickly gain confidence in making your shots.

6. Competitiveness

Ray Worters, all-star goal-keeper, of hockey fame, who minded the nets for the New York Americans in the 30's, revealed to me during a brief chat in Toronto that before any important game he could not keep food on his stomach. Jimmy Ward, former star defenceman with the Montreal Maroons, said, "I wouldn't want to be on the same team with a player who didn't have butterflies in his stomach before an important game." These statements, coming from men of proven competitive spirit, made me feel a lot better. For years I had considered myself one of those unhealthy specimens of humanity who had a weak stomach. During any bonspiel or playdown I had always had trouble eating heartily and during the last few days of an important championship, nothing other than liquids would remain in my stomach. Sometimes I wonder whether this so-called competitive stomach is worth the shot, yet I remember reading Bobby Jones's book on golf where he mentioned being so nervous and upset on the day of the final match that he couldn't put a knot in his tie.

Competitiveness seems to be a determination or a desire to excel or the "will-to-win". There is nothing wrong with wanting to be a winner; to do better than the next man. That is the basis of our system of free enterprise to-day.

Sportsmanship must enter the picture, too. That is one reason why curling is such a grand game. There is no room in it for the poor sport. When automobile bonspiels were first proposed, the cry went up that the sportsmanship would be taken out of curling when players were competing for such valuable prizes. Such was not the case. Curling is too strong an institution, and good sportsmanship is too well engrained in good curlers, to encourage unethical practices no matter how valuable the prize may be.

7. Consistency

The steady, dependable player is of far more value to a rink than a brilliant but inconsistent one. The temperament of a person often enters into his reliability or steadiness. The impulsive individual is a gambler by nature and would rather hazard a shot that could produce big dividends than one where the law of averages was in his favour.

A curler will be more consistent if there is less variation in the type of shot or weight he plays. A chap-and-lie game makes for more consistency than the running game because the player is using draw weight or a little over draw for passing through opponents' rocks.

Practice and experience help to develop consistency, and when self-control and sound judgment are added, you will find a curler who will make a good percentage of his shots in any game he plays. When you get a combination of four men on a team playing consistently, making at least six shots out of eight on each end with monotonous regularity, the morale of the opposing team will show signs of ripping at the seams. Sometimes it doesn't happen till well toward the end of a game, but eventually the tide will turn. One game in particular I shall remember as long as I live. We were playing in the City Championship against Stan Speers of the Fort Rouge Club. End after end we had built up good "heads" but each time Stan would freeze to one of our shot stones and, try as I might, I couldn't get his rock out far enough to score a "big end". This went on to the eleventh end; my boys were still drawing them in, even after all the heartbreaks of earlier attempts. Finally Stan missed his last rock and the "big five" that we had been working for all through the game, materialized. We were just "kids" at that time, but it was a very valuable lesson that we never forgot.

CHAPTER 4

Strategy in Skipping

I think it was in 1927 that I was given a first class lesson in skipping strategy that I shall never forget. Our "kid rink" was breezing through the Winnipeg Bonspiel at a merry clip. We had reached the "eights" of all three major competitions undefeated, when we ran smack into R. J. "Bob" Gourlay, as clever an ice strategist as there was. We were scheduled to play R. J. on two successive draws at the Thistle Curling Club at 4:00 P.M. and again at 8:00 P.M. That year all five sheets of ice at the Thistle were concave or "dished", as curlers say. That is, the centre of each sheet was hollowed from one end to the other, and the side ice was so much higher that no matter what turn you played, or what ice the skip gave, every stone fell back to the centre line if it was a guard or draw. Bob Gourlay sized up the sheet after a few stones had been played and from then on adopted the strategy of playing his stones in front of the "house". Foolishly we tried to draw behind these stones and succeeded only in raising them to the house. The more ice we took the more our stones fell back, and try as we might, we couldn't get anywhere. The first game we absorbed a severe trouncing. In the second game we began to catch onto R. J.'s strategy about the sixth end, but it was too late. The heart had been taken out of us, and we took the short end of the count again. I honestly believe that we were playing the broom and the weight more accurately than our opposition, but R. J. Gourlay was using his head and making the most of every shot. Next day we lost another game and found ourselves out of the 'spiel, but the lessons learned stood us in good stead and won many games for us in later years.

Many, many times I have seen a rink play well-nigh flawlessly, and its skip use excellent judgment in planning the ends right up to the last part of the game. Then suddenly, at a time when a crucial shot required sound judgment, the skip suffered a lapse of memory, or gave in to impulse, and called for a shot that got him into trouble, and eventually cost the game. Too often this happens on the last end during a close match, and all the good play and hard sweeping of his team goes for nought. A high-class skipper requires more than playmaking ability and ability to read ice. He is the field marshal for his team, and his generalship calls for sound decisions in strategy based on foresight, a sense of anticipation, and a thorough knowledge of the fundamentals of skipping.

This chapter is primarily for the skip and for those who aspire to his unenviable position. It is impossible to cover all situations that a skip might be confronted with, but I shall attempt to make a searching analysis of all the major fundamentals involved in skipping strategy under a variety of conditions. Remember—there are exceptions to every rule, only experience, combined with alertness, opportunism, and courage, will dictate the proper action when such exceptions arise. One of the reasons why curling holds such fascination for its adherents is because of the amazing number of situations that can arise in a given number of games played. With sixteen stones in play each end, no two ends will present problems exactly alike. This adds fuel to the locker-room post-mortems and provides endless material for heated discussions by the "perfectionists" behind the glass, or the participants after the game. The old question asked a million times a year: "Why did you play that shot on the —th end?" will never be worn out as long as curling exists. It would require another volume to try to answer all questions that might arise in this connection. It must suffice here to study general patterns that beset the average skip and, even with that, some of my evaluations will naturally be open to rebuttal, as they represent my own personal opinions, which may not necessarily be those of many other skips.

JUDGING ICE FOR THE PLAYER

There is no weakness in a skip that causes his players to lose confidence in him more quickly than his inability to read ice correctly. This is of particular importance during the first few ends of a game in order to get away to a good start. Every skip should watch the ice very carefully the first two ends. Here are a few hints that may help:

Judging Ice During Early Stages of a Game

1. If at all possible, have your lead play both turns the first and second end, an in-turn on one side of the sheet, and an out-turn on the other. These two experiments should give you a fair idea of how the ice "works".

2. Watch both stones played by the opposing lead and the amount of ice he actually took (not the ice given by his skip). Determine whether he was wide or narrow of the broom and how far his stone "pulled" for the weight he used.

3. Observe carefully where the stones of both lead men stop in relation to the amount of ice they took to get there.

4. During the first few ends concentrate on watching each stone played by your men for direction only. Let your sweepers judge the weight. Your job as skip during the early ends is to "read" the ice and detect every wrinkle on its surface. This is very important. You can not do it if you are sweeping.

5. Stand back at the tee-line and watch each stone for direction. Resist the temptation to run out to sweep.

6. Make mental notes, on every shot played, of the amount of "pull" for each turn on at least five areas of the ice; centre, right and left of centre, and on the left and right sides of the sheet. Store this information in your mind and memorize it.

7. Where the ice has been hand-pebbled, your stones will draw less the first end or two until the pebble wears off. Play your take-out shots firmly with very little ice. By firmly, I mean hack-weight, which will not draw very much on normal ice the first end or two.

8. Do not hesitate to experiment with a draw shot by your lead or second over an unplayed area to guard against a roll to that area by your opponent. It can be too costly for the third or skip to guess at the amount of ice when they play their shots.

9. By the time several shots have been played in each of the first two ends, you should have in your mind a blueprint of the ice registered. So instead of watching that game on the next sheet, memorize the blueprint until it is indelibly impressed. This blueprint should actually be three-dimensional, like a relief map. Depth or contours of the ice surface are as important as its length and width.

Depth perception is a skill possessed by few skips. A good skip will know the exact location of every ridge and hollow on the ice. He will have these visualized in his mind and so well charted that he will know exactly what ridges and hollows his player's stone will have to pass over on its course down the ice. Therefore, he knows what ice to give, and this uncanny ability distinguishes him from other skips when playing on "tricky" ice.

Judging Ice During the Later Stages of a Game

A skip must ever be on the alert for changing ice conditions during the progress of a game whether he is playing on artificial ice or natural ice. Air temperature changes affect ice surface quickly, and every change in the condition of the ice means a change in the amount of "broom" required in giving ice to the players for their shots. This means that the skip cannot relax his vigilance in watching the action of every stone played.

During play in the second last match in the Canadian Curling Championships at Hamilton, in March, 1949, the square pebble, which had been put on by machine the day before, began to wear off. About the seventh end in this game against Pete Gilbert and his Ontario rink, the ice had become much keener than it had been two or three ends earlier. All rocks were "pulling" more as the game progressed. I suppose I had become a bit complacent as the score was 10-3 in our favour, for I had failed to notice the change. We had three "seconds" in the rings when I went to play the last stone of the seventh end. I took the usual amount of ice to pass through Pete's only shot. I played the weight and broom perfectly, but my stone drew a foot more than I anticipated, and instead of our counting four, Ontario scored one. From then on we had our hands full to pull out of that game on the winning side. One miss through carelessness could have cost us the game. It upset my confidence and I curled erratically the last few ends. I could recount dozens of such experiences, but I shall have to confine myself to admonishing all skips to keep a weather-eye out for the following situations:

1. Gradual wearing of the pebble on the outside as well as the centre of the sheet, will call for more ice.

2. "Swingy" or wet ice will gradually dry up if temperatures

outside the rink are dropping. This calls for less ice. Similarly, in artificial ice plants, when the power is increased, the ice will harden so that less ice is required.

3. On frosty ice, the opposite is true. When temperatures are rising outside, the ice becomes keener and the rocks "pull" more. On artificial ice, sometimes the plant is turned off for an hour or so, causing the ice to get keener or "swingy".

4. During championship match play, the body temperatures from the crowds of people affect the ice surface.

5. On "tricky" ice, where the stone falls against the turn, or runs straight, there is even greater danger in giving ice when the temperature in the rink is changing.

6. On a cold night when the temperature is dropping, it does so more rapidly after the players have gone back into the clubrooms. If you and your opponents are still playing after the other teams have left the ice, then watch your broom and your weight very carefully, as the ice surface will frost quickly.

7. Where the "plant" is suddenly switched off in artificial ice rinks, the fun really starts in an end or two. Many games considered won at this point have been lost in the last ends when the ice becomes very "swingy" and more and more ice has to be given for an ordinary take-out shot. When the condition of the ice changes radically, the type of game played should undergo a change, too, as well as the amount of ice given.

It all boils down to one thing: Irrespective of the stage of the game, whether early or late, *a smart skip is always watchful.* No matter what the score, whether he is five down or twelve up, he cannot afford to grow careless. One mental slip will upset the whole rink.

Allowing for Peculiarities of Delivery

Any skip knows that no two men deliver a stone alike. Each player has his own method, however slightly it may differ from another's. Here are some of the peculiarities and the allowance that must be made in each case:

1. In-turn "hooked" out—requires less ice

This is an in-turn swing inside the direct line to the skip's broom which the player tries to correct by "hooking" or pushing the stone towards the broom.

2. In-turn "pushed" or "steered" in—requires more ice

Here the swing is outside the correct line to the broom, and the player at the moment of release "steers" or "pushes" his stone towards the skip's broom.

3. Out-turn "hooked" out—requires less ice

This is the same action as described with the in-turn (stone is swung inside the correct line).

4. Out-turn "pushed" or "steered" in—requires more ice

The line of swing is outside the broom, in this case, and the player is attempting to correct his line.

5. A spinning handle—requires less ice

6. A slow turning handle—requires more ice

7. A "wobbler"—requires much less ice

JUDGING WEIGHT AND DIRECTION

As the skip directs all play from his position on the "head", except when playing his own stones, he must, of necessity, be a good judge of weight in guiding his sweepers, and he must also keep himself in a position from which he can watch the approaching stone so that it can be directed to its proper destination.

A skip cannot be too careful in judging the weight of a draw shot because, if he is playing against a top-notch rink, positional play of every rock is vital. If at all possible, he will want his stones lined up in the circles to prevent double take-outs by his opponent. He will watch the weight of a guard rock like a hawk, calling for sweeping if necessary so that it comes to rest at the spot where it will be the most formidable. He will have his sweepers nurse a slowly moving stone until it stops exactly on the spot he desires, not half a foot short or a few inches too far. Too many skips are happy to get a rock within a foot or two of where they want it, then they wonder why their luck is so bad when a smart opponent sees an opening, plays his shot perfectly, and thus spoils what looked like a big end.

One very costly lesson taught me to keep my eye on the stone and watch its weight. It happened in the Canadian Brier Finals, too. At Quebec City in 1942, playing Alberta, we were one down, playing the tenth end. Alberta was lying two when I played my last stone. I elected to draw to the four-foot circle to try to count one and tie the score on that crucial end. At the second hog my draw seemed light, and in my anxiety I moved in to help the boys sweep. Brother Grant came out from the "head" too, and not until the stone had reached the twelve foot ring did we realize that there was plenty of weight. We all ceased sweeping and the stone moved to the tee-line where the Alberta third man, who was a powerful sweeper, "took hold" of it and on the keen ice managed to sweep it back to the eight foot circle, thus leaving their two stones counting. That put us three down. We got one back on the eleventh and were two down coming home. Grant had to make two of the most brilliant shots of his career to pull the game out of the fire for us on the home end. Without these we actually had lost the game on the tenth end, through lack of care in judging weight. It might interest you to know that, since 1942 I have swept my own rock on only one occasion.

The foregoing story illustrates the necessity of a skip being on the job at all times in judging weight. The same applies to watching direction. Look over the following hints and check yourself next time you play:

Stand or crouch at the tee and on the line of direction for:

(a) A take-out
(b) Passing a guard
(c) Guarding the "shot"
(d) Negotiating a port
(e) Raising one of your own stones
(f) Playing an in or out wick

And stay there until the shot is completed. Resist the urge to draw off to one side (as if to help pull the stone in the right direction). A captain stays with his ship. Do likewise. Even though the stone appears to need help in sweeping, you'll gain more if you stay back and direct the sweepers. Only on very rare occasions does a skipper leave his post:

(a) In case of a simple draw, where weight is the only considera-tion
(b) To help pull a guard over the last few inches when you

know your sweepers are exhausted and have no more power
in their strokes

(c) To get a guard over the hog line

(d) To sweep behind the tee

(e) To sweep in one of your own stones that is moved by an
unforeseen "fluke" or lucky shot. A sense of anticipation
will help in this case

All do's and dont's apply similarly to the third, or vice-skip,
when he is in charge of the "head".

In the case of a shot which requires judgment of both weight
and direction, the skip (or the man on the tee line) should be
responsible for direction and the sweepers, or the player following
the stone, should watch the weight.

SKIPPING STRATEGY—THE FIRST END

These days, when entry lists are overcrowded, many Bonspiel
Committees reduce the length of the games to ten ends. In a twelve
end game you can occasionally afford to get off to a bad start and
still pull the chestnuts out of the fire, but in a ten-end match you
have got to get started on the right foot. Strategy then, for that first
end, is of much concern to many skips.

There are several considerations that have a bearing on the
results of the first end: (a) the ability of your team, and particularly
your lead, to "catch" draw weight; (b) the ability of the skip to
size up the ice; (c) the skip's strategy; (d) the opponent's strategy.
Of these the first two have been discussed in detail, whereas the last
must be considered in examining the third. The first questions that
most skips want an answer for is, "Where should I place the first
stone?"

Position of the First Stone

We will assume that your side has lost the toss and your lead is
in the hack ready to deliver his first stone. Let us also assume that
you are playing on good ice. There are two schools of opinion.

    1. Place it in front of the rings

    2. Place it in or on the rings

The first group uses the logic that when your opponent has last
rock you will have to have guards in front to roll behind, or draw

behind, to make it difficult for the opposition to count one, even with last rock in their favour. The second group argues that if you play your first in front, your opponent can use it for cover as much as you can, and it may be the cause of the opposition scoring three or four on the first end instead of one.

For years my eldest sister was a faithful supporter at most of our games, and one question she asked year after year was: "Why do you waste a rock by putting it in front of the rings? It will never count out there." I scoffed at her criticism and dismissed the question with: "We put it there to draw behind or roll behind. Anyway, what do you know about skipping?" This went on for years, and she still asked the same question. Finally, about 1943-4, my brother Grant began to wonder, too, and he tried to convince me of the fallacy. He did persuade me to discard the idea against some rinks whom we considered poor hitters, then suddenly it dawned on me that our thinking had been wrong all those years. What is a rock in the front but a hedge against the opposing skip making his last shot! We were automatically conceding his ability to make that last shot. In other words, we were using defensive strategy instead of assuming the offensive right from the starting bell. So we tried the experiment of placing the first stone in the house instead. (We had lots of opportunity to do so, for I think we have lost 70% of the tosses of the coin during the last few years.) The general result was, that, in the majority of our bonspiel games, we counted from two to five points on that first end. The opposing skip wasn't always making the shots we had originally given him credit for.

Now after twenty or more years of arguing in favour of placing the first stone in front, I find myself in the opposite camp with those who want to draw to the rings instead. Let me give you further reasons for this decision:

1. It aids the lead to get the feel of draw weight immediately, which he never does when placing the first stone in front.

2. It puts the other skip on the defensive immediately.

3. If the opposition is guilty of two or three misses so that you are lying two or three when you play your last stone, play a short guard on the key rock and make it difficult for him to count.

4. The average lead man is not a strong "hitter", therefore he is playing his most difficult shot when your lead draws in to the rings. If, however, you played out in front, the opposing lead has only to play his specialty, which is a draw.

5. Similarly, if your lead is not a strong hitter, why wait to put him in that position first instead of the opposing lead?

6. You will learn more about how the ice "works" if the first stone travels all the way to the rings.

7. Drawing around guards is a particularly difficult shot the first end.

But as in every rule, there are exceptions:

1. If you know your opposing skip well enough to know that a rock out in front worries him, then put it there, or if two rocks out in front worry him even more, put two of them there.

2. Against a strong lead who is an accurate hitter, place the first stone three or four feet in front of the rings.

3. On ice that has a natural hollow in centre so that it is impossible to draw around a stone in front of the house, place your first rock in front.

4. If your players are poor hitters, there is an excuse for placing the first stone in front.

Where in the Rings Should the First Stone be Placed?

If you decide to draw into the rings with the first stone on the first end, when you are not certain how the ice "works", use centre ice for the in- or out-turn, preferably the out-turn, which is usually harder for the average lead to hit. If possible, sweep this stone to the tee line or just behind so that there is less chance for a roll to the other side of the house, where you are not familiar with the ice.

If it is a sheet of ice you know fairly well, try to draw it to the eight-foot or twelve-foot circle (see Fig. 61), or if you are aware that there is a "tricky run" in the ice, try to place it on the "sidehill" of that "run".

Placing the Stone in Front of the Rings　(See Fig. 61)

Should you decide to place a stone out in front, the best position would be on or close to the centre line about three or four feet in front of the twelve-foot circle for the following reasons:

1. A stone just in front of the house is in a strategic position for a raise or as a guard to roll behind.

2. If too far out in front, it has only a nuisance value as it is not a good guard nor can it be raised easily.

3. If too close to the twelve-foot or "biting" the outer circle, it provides the opportunity for the opposition to hit it and role to the side of the house.

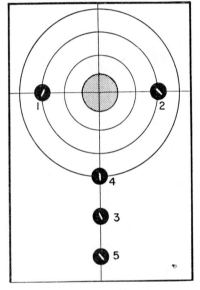

FIG. 61

Placing the first stone in the first end:

1. Out-turn draw
2. In-turn draw
3. In front of the rings
4. Biting front ring
5. Long guard

Listed in order of preference.

4. If the stone is on the centre line, you can play on either side of it and find out how the ice "works". But if the stone is in front but to one side, it blocks off most of the play to that side of the house.

After the First Stone Has Been Played

If the opposition has played the first stone in front of the rings, do not try to draw in behind it. Reserve this strategy for later in the game when your players are sure of draw weight. If your lead attempts to draw behind it he will usually be short and you will have the front of the house "plugged" before you know it, thus making it difficult for you to use your last rock effectively. If possible, have your lead draw to the side of the house on or behind the tee line between the eight- and twelve-foot rings (see Fig. 61). Try not to let it rest on the twelve-foot at the 7 or 8 o'clock position (see Fig. 62), or it will be in perfect position for the opposition to hit it and roll in behind the stone in front of the rings. Either sweep it back to the tee or let it stop one or two feet short of the rings where it can be raised to the house.

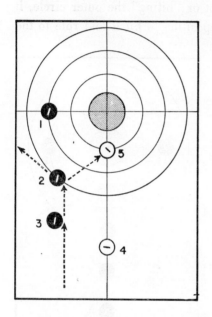

FIG. 62

After the first stone (No. 4) has been played by the opposition, play your lead stone to No. 1 position, or No. 3. In No. 2 it affords a chance for the opposing team to strike it and roll to No. 5 position where it will be well protected, and difficult to remove. A stone stopping at No. 3 will not be so vulnerable, and may be raised later.

Avoid having your men play over-weight or heavy hack-weight shots the first end unless the front of the house becomes so "plugged" that it is absolutely necessary. Try to get the other rink to do all the hitting the first end or two. Thus while your men are getting the feel of draw weight, the opposing team have no opportunity to do so.

During the first few ends, try to keep your opponent hitting while you are exploring every nook and cranny in the sheet of ice, and giving your men a chance to get their weight. Let the other skip do the gambling while you are playing the percentage shots. If you jump into a lead the first end or two, do not start to protect it by guarding every "shot" rock. Keep spreading your draw shots around the rings to maintain the pressure.

STRATEGY IN PLAY

There are so many types of shots called for in a match that it seems advisable to classify them and deal with the principles of strategy involved for each one. Bear in mind that the abilities of your players must be given consideration when considering the type of shot to be played. In each of the following cases, I am assuming that your player can make the shot called for.

When to Draw

There are countless times when every skip has gone into a mental huddle with himself, or his vice-skip, to make a decision whether to draw, guard, strike, or raise. Personally, I have watched consultations lasting from five to ten minutes over a simple choice of whether to hit or to draw. Many of these sessions are needless and the longer the deliberation, the less likelihood of the shot being made, for no player can execute a shot when there is uncertainty in his mind. Here are my conclusions concerning such situations:

1. If you are the shotmaker, play the draw if you have more confidence in that shot.

2. The farther back the opponent's stone is, the quieter the weight to be played. If his stone is on the back rings, draw to it. The chances of hitting and "sticking" are slim. Besides, if you draw to the face of it or in front of it, you automatically provide backing for your stone (see Fig. 63).

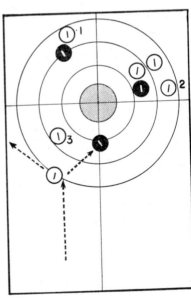

FIG. 63

Play a draw when your opponent's stones are in any of the following positions:

1. On the back ring.
2. In a pocket.
3. Partially guarded.

3. Draw to any pocket of stones behind the tee line unless it is absolutely necessary to move one of the stones back to increase your number of "counters".

4. Use draw or back-ring weight if only the corner of a stone you want to move is exposed (see Fig. 63). As the chances of making

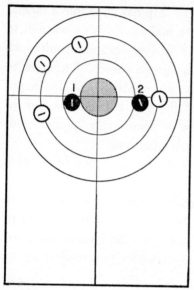

FIG. 64

It is preferable not to guard No. 1 but draw to No. 2 position for second shot.

the shot perfectly are slim, you will get a shot almost as effective by chipping the guard and rolling quietly to another part of the house, at the same time exposing the stone you were trying to move.

5. The best guard is second shot. Even though the opposition has last rock, if you lie one shot on the side rings, draw to the other side of the house for a second.

6. If you have shot rock and your opponent has three or four seconds, draw for second shot well away from your first. A guard is one of the hardest shots to execute well (see Fig. 64). This will prevent many a big end being scored against you.

7. When you are three or four points down you cannot afford to do too much hitting. Play the draw game and wait for a break that will give you an opportunity for a big end.

8. Play a draw around a long guard, but hit a short guard.

9. A skip should normally prefer a draw with his last stone, or

no more than over-draw weight. He must save his stones at all costs as they are of no value behind the rings. If the opponent has shot rock, play to move it back quietly so that if you only get a "piece" of his stone, your rock will still be in the rings. This keeps the pressure on the other skip to remove your stone in order to score. If you have last stone, it is all the more imperative that you save your rock by playing quiet weight except under unusual circumstances. Fig. 65 illustrates a situation where many skips flounder. It does not require much mental arithmetic to figure out that, if your opponents score three instead of your scoring one, a difference of four points registers on the score-board. The larger the number of stones your opponents have in the rings when you play your last stone, the quieter your weight should be. Even if you have lots of backing, stick to a quiet "over-tee" weight. If you are several points ahead at the time, your duty is to play for one more, not to play to cut the end down.

FIG. 65

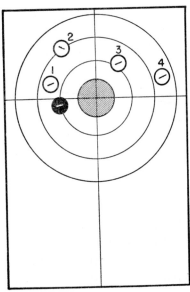

Play your last stone quietly with little more than "over-tee" weight. Preferably if there is a pocket (formed by stones 1 and 2) you have two chances for backing to save or cut down the end. Playing to No. 3 stone is more hazardous. On no account play a wick shot from No. 1 to No. 3 even though the opposing skip has last stone. If stone No. 2 were missing, a choice would exist between drawing to No. 1 or No. 3. Then use the turn that gives you the better chance.

10. There are times when your rink has built up a big end only to have the opposing skip spoil it by playing a freeze or partial-freeze shot. Then you will have to resist the urge to try to smash his out to salvage part of the big end. This is where the experienced

skip restrains his impulsiveness, and, if the game is close, or if he is up a few points, he will play a draw and be satisfied with one or two. This situation arose in the tenth end of the only game we lost during the 1936 Canadian Championships. We were two down playing Emmett Smith, Northern Ontario representative. We lay five when Emmett played a beautiful freeze with his last stone. After his shot we still lay one, but I was determined to squeeze his stone out with a running shot. It had to be a fine shot to move him, and I missed and nicked out our only shot in so doing. This gave Northern Ontario one when I could have drawn in for two and tied the game. Fig. 66 illustrates the positions of the stones when I made this error.

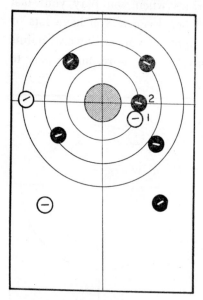

FIG. 66

Here is the situation that existed in the tenth end of a game with Northern Ontario. There is still one "black" rock to play. The correct play is to draw for two points, as No. 2 is shot rock. If you were several points down, you would have to gamble on chipping out No. 1.

When to Guard

In an offensive style of play, a guard is the last type of shot to use, but there are occasions when it is a "must", even though you have last rock. It is important, too, to know when to play short guards, long guards, or middle-length guards. A guard is a protector and should be used only when no other shot would improve your position, or when one or two of your stones are in such vulnerable places that you are "sticking your neck out" by not preserving your advantage. I do not refer to the skip who, immediately he gets a shot stone in

the rings begins to "guard the living daylights out of it" so that he
will not have to use his last rock. Such strategy is closely akin to
that of the proverbial ostrich sticking his head in the sand. If a skip
hasn't got the courage to try to make his last stone count, he should
relinquish his position to someone who has. Guards may be excused
under the following circumstances:

1. To protect the possibility of a double take-out by a rink of
sharp-shooters, and this only in the later stages of the end.

2. To protect a possible roll off the key rock into a nest of your
own rocks which may be well hidden by stones in front of the house
(see Fig. 67).

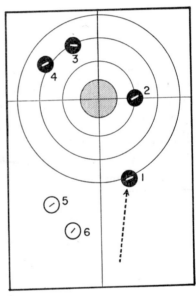

FIG. 67

A medium guard (No. 1) is called
for in this situation where a roll by
the opponent in behind 5 and 6 and
in front of 3 and 4 would be disastrous to the end. If it were too close
to No. 2, the same situation would
exist and, if too long, it would only
have a nuisance value. Notice that
the guard (No. 1) is inside and closer
to the centre line than No. 2. Only
the outside edge of No. 2 is exposed.
If the opposition did play the out-
turn past No. 1, their stone would
still remain exposed if it struck No. 2.

3. In building a good-sized end, it is often necessary for the skip
to guard the key rock to protect the position of the other stone. In
this case, a short guard is called for (see Fig. 68). A short guard is
close enough to use in a "raise" if any damage is done by the other
skip's stone. In addition, it puts another "counter" in the rings and
thereby adds to the worries of the opposition.

4. A long guard is necessary in the last resort to block a raise
or "close" a port. Quite often the front of the house becomes so
cluttered with rocks that there is no alternative but to protect the

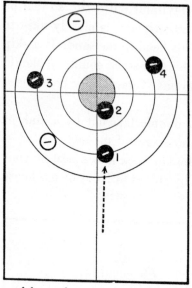

FIG. 68

No. 2 is in a bad position for a roll by the opposition towards No. 3, or in front of No. 4. A close guard (No. 1) adds a fourth counter but is far enough in front to prevent any gain from hitting it. The opposing skip has no alternative but to draw or hit No. 1. The position of the guard gives him a very difficult shot in any event.

position of your shot rocks in the rings. If you lie one and your opposition has three or four seconds and it is impossible to draw for second shot, you have only one recourse, and that is to guard. Fig. 69 illustrates a situation in which a long guard is called for.

5. If you have a lead of several points in a game, do not hesitate to guard second shot or even third shot if circumstances warrant it.

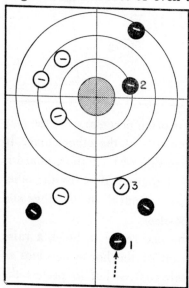

FIG. 69

No. 2 is shot, and it is difficult to draw for second shot. In addition No. 3 is in a good position for a raise to score a big end for the opposition. A long guard (No. 1) protects the raise and if this is your last stone, the other skip will have to draw for one, or play a long-odds shot for a big end.

If No. 3 rock were on the eight foot ring or closer, the same shot would be called for.

If your opponents have a "houseful" of stones and your stone is second shot and inaccessible, do not take any chance of exposing it. Here is an illustration of a shot that cost us a game in the St. Paul Midsummer Bonspiel. We were five up, playing the eleventh end at the time (see Fig. 70).

FIG. 70

No. 1 is second shot. No. 2 was played into the house at my request by my third man. I had hoped to place it further back and more to the right side of the rings. The opposing skip had now a perfect set up for a wick shot from 2 to 1. He made it perfectly, and they lay five. Subsequent shots failed to change the picture and Elmer Freytag of Chicago counted a big five to tie the game. He scored one on the last end to win. The logical shot was to place a guard in No. 3 position and the five end could not have been scored.

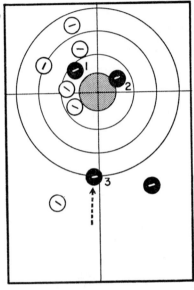

6. When your opponent has last stone, there are times, even when he has shot rock, when you come to play your last stone, that it is wise to guard and prevent his being able to draw for two rather than try to get "shot" yourself. I have been faced with this problem many times, the last occasion took place at the Thistle Club in Hamilton, Ontario, in the 1949 Brier Playdowns in the final game against Reg Stone, of the British Columbia rink. We were both undefeated and the score was 10-6 in our favour, playing the eleventh end. Reg had just made a beautiful out-turn draw on side ice to get shot rock. Here is the problem that faced me when I came to throw my last stone in that end. Reg. still had another to play (see Fig. 71).

When to Use the "Chap and Lie"

"Chap and lie" weight should be used in 75% of your take-out shots. It is the safest and most reliable shot to use as the weight required is little more than enough to remove an opposing stone from the rings. Sometimes it is referred to as "light-hack" weight, which is just sufficient weight for a rock to reach the hack. The adoption of this type of play by a rink will enable it to score many "big ends" in a season's play as the stones used in removing an opponent's will seldom roll out of the rings.

Players can be much more accurate playing "chap and lie" weight on normal ice because they have time to settle down in the follow-through; also it is easier for them to gauge the weight as it is only

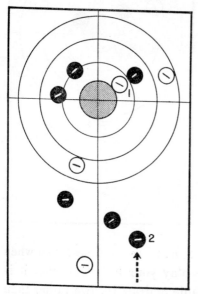

FIG. 71

In this situation, with last rock against us and a lead of a few points, it was wise to guard against the opposing skip drawing for second shot. No. 1 is the shot stone, so No. 2 was played to prevent any chance of the opposition scoring two on this end. The ice in this game was tricky and there was no need to risk taking out No. 1 when a long or short guard would eliminate any chance of scoring more than one.

eighteen feet heavier than tee-line weight. The latter is the basis on which the weight required in most shots is calculated. Once a curler starts throwing over-weight shots, he finds it more difficult to revert to draw weight again. "Chap and lie" weight is used by most top-notch rinks in Manitoba, Alberta, and British Columbia. Saskatchewan curlers favour the running game more because ice surface conditions in rinks in many parts of that province are not conducive to quieter weight. The same applies in many rural areas in Manitoba where keen ice does not prevail. Keen ice is necessary in order to play the "chap and lie" weight effectively. This means that the side ice as well as centre ice must allow the rocks to run easily, and it also explains why different styles of games are prevalent in different parts of the country. The Canadian Curling Championships are always played on artificial ice which is normally keen, therefore the exponents of the "chap and lie", and those experienced in its use, usually have an advantage over those who favour the "running" game or the draw style.

Use the "chap and lie" weight, then:

1. If the ice surface is keen

2. When removing one stone from the rings

3. For maintaining your draw weight

4. For saving your stones and building up an end

5. For rolling into the rings off a stone one or two feet in front of the house

6. To play a wick and roll

7. To maintain steady accurate play when you are well up in score during the middle or late stages of your match

8. To keep the feel of draw-weight and carry it over to the next game during bonspiel play.

When to Play a Raise

Gordon Hudson used to catch me napping on occasions when he asked his lead or second to play a draw about two or three feet short of the house to the right or left of centre. It was just far enough out of the house so that we couldn't get a roll into the rings from it. So I would call for a draw to the house on the other side of the sheet. Then when we missed a shot, Gordon calmly walked over to his stone in front of the house and gave the "raise" signal to his player. Once the stone was raised to the rings, it not only was a counter, but usually it was guarded as well. He caught me two or three times with that before I became smart enough to know why he wanted it there. Henceforth it was promptly removed before any trouble brewed (see Fig. 72).

A raise is good strategy when you find these situations:

1. When the ice is "grooved" or runs fairly straight, a short or even a middle length raise is advisable.

2. When the opponent is shot and guarded by one of your stones, play the raise with no more than light-hack weight. If you don't

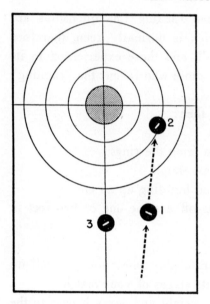

FIG. 72

A stone placed in the No. 1 position is handy for a raise to No. 2 where it is shot and guarded.

If your stone was placed just as illustrated by No. 3, a good opposing skip would remove it immediately. Use the strategy as shown by Nos. 1 and 2 when you have last rock. You will often score two by this ruse.

succeed in raising it "dead on" you will at least have removed the guard. "Back-ring" weight is good strategy for such a raise when you have a few of your own rocks in the house as seconds. You will not disturb these seconds and you will have pushed another of your stones into the house.

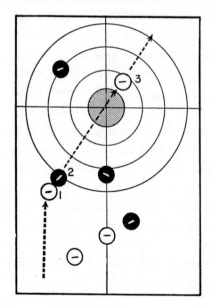

FIG. 73

A Combination Raise

Here is a perfect set up for removing the "shot" stone to lie three counters. If No. 1 stone is hit almost anywhere, it will drive No. 2 against No. 3.

Many combinations like this are usable if you are alert to them, but do not make the mistake of trying this type of shot unless you are absolutely certain the angle is correct.

3. Raise a stone whether your own or your opponent's, anytime the ice is such that you cannot draw around it. If it is an opposing rock, use enough weight to raise it through the house.

4. The longer the raise, the less chance of making it. Draw around a long guard every time when it is possible to do so. A raise is one of the most difficult shots in curling. If it is necessary to use heavy ice at the sides to get around a long guard, you have no alternative but to raise it.

5. Watch closely for combinations of stones on the front rings or in front of the house. They often afford excellent possibilities for a raise when a clear shot is not available. Stones that are "frozen", or almost so, whether in line with each other or on an angle, provide opportunities that will get you out of many serious situations (see Fig. 73).

6. Remember that a double or triple raise involving two or more stones requires more weight to move them. If a double-angular raise is played it will require even more weight, particularly if the first stone struck has to clip the corner of a second stone which is the one you actually desire to move.

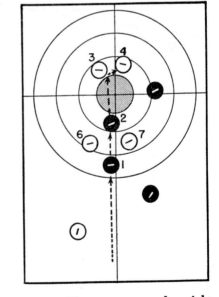

FIG. 74

Another Combination

This unusual shot was executed during a club game in Winnipeg several years ago. The position of the rocks makes it almost impossible to miss if No. 1 stone is struck squarely. There was a difference of five points involved in the score. The "whites" lay two before the shot, and the "blacks" have three counters when the smoke clears away.

Even if stone No. 1 was hit slightly on one side, it would carom off Nos. 6 and 7, but would follow through to strike No. 2, which would finish the job even though it struck No. 4 stone first. Nor was too much weight used to complete this shot.

When to Play a Roll

There are several good reasons why it pays to try for a roll when striking the opposing stones:

1. To keep from bunching your own stones in the rings
2. To "bury" your stone behind a guard
3. To get your stone in front of opposing rocks for "backing"
4. To execute double take-outs
5. To roll to a position guarding another stone
6. To change play from one side of the "house" to the other during the early ends so that the opposing skip will have more difficulty in judging the run of the ice.

Continual change of position of your stones tends to confuse the other skip. He has continually to readjust his strategy to meet the new situation. Watch the rolls carefully. Play for them by taking the exact amount of ice needed to produce the roll. Direct your sweepers accordingly. Be alert and ready with your own broom to help your stones roll to the position you desire, and sweep vigorously if necessary. Lots of action and quick-thinking on the "head" will often rattle the other skip. Have all possible results worked out in your mind before the shot is played, then you will anticipate anything that might happen.

Fig. 75 illustrates a case in point.

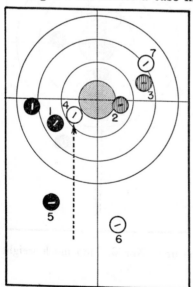

FIG. 75

Getting a Roll

No. 4 stone is to be removed. There are several possibilities as illustrated by the positions Nos. 1, 2 and 3.

No. 1—Striking the outside of No. 4 and rolling behind the guard No. 5.

No. 2—Striking the inside of No. 4 and rolling behind the guard No. 6.

No. 3—Striking the inside of No. 4 and rolling back to the face of No. 7.

Striking the rock and getting no roll would be the least effective shot of the four.

Removing Guards

Stones have a bad habit of stopping in front of the rings and, being made of granite seven inches high and a foot wide, when several of them congregate they can be pretty formidable obstacles. As there is no such thing as a drop-kick in curling, and as players are not permitted to throw their stones overhand, guards have to be removed if you want to clear an open road to the "house".

A common conception, prevalent among skips and curlers alike, is that guards can be removed by blasting at them with a runner, hurled with all the physical might of the player, in the general direction of the offending granites. As the stone hurtles down the ice like a ball shot out of a cannon, skips and players jump for safety, close their eyes, hold their hands over their ears, turn their backs, and hunch their shoulders in expectancy of the explosive blast that is supposed to take place. But instead of the air being filled with flying pieces of granite, usually there is a dull "crack" and a boom as one of the maze of rocks is buffeted from its place to hit the boards at the back. When eyes are opened they find unbelievingly little or no sign of destruction.

We have the same futile application of brute strength exhibited when the dub golfer finds himself in a deep sand trap. Explosion shots in golf and removing of guards in curling require study and scientific precision in executing the shot. Most curlers forget that granite is resilient, therefore a "runner" will not push rocks aside as it would an army of wooden soldiers. One well directed hack-weight shot will do more to remove a few guards than all the blindly thrown runners in the world. First select the guard you want to hit and where you want to hit it to move other guards, then put the broom down for the ice required to do the job. Get into the hack; get set for your delivery, blot all other rocks out of your mind except the one you are trying to hit; decide what weight you are going to play, then concentrate on swinging at the broom. This is where a good third man comes in handy. In my estimation, my brother Grant, and "Bung" Cartmell, who played third rock for Ab Gowanlock of Glenboro, are the best "clean up" men that I have seen in the curling game. They both select the shot and have the ability to shoot for the corners of the rock they want to strike first.

The diatribe above is concerned mostly with "opening up" the front of the house, but the same admonition can be applied to removing single stones, or making simple doubles where two guards are closer together. There is not much use removing a guard if your stone replaces it. The problem is to remove both stones and that means aiming for the corners.

Keep these thoughts in mind when removing guards:

1. Play no more weight than a firm heavy-hack or you will throw yourself off the line of delivery.

2. Swing at the broom and blot the rock out of your mind.

3. Use the turn that pulls most when removing a guard, or at least a turn that pulls a foot or two. If you use a straight run in the ice you will likely hit the guard full and "stick".

4. If two guards are involved make certain you remove the one that is the more troublesome. That is, open up the side where the ice "pulls", not the side where there is a run. It is easy for the opposition to replace a guard located on a "run".

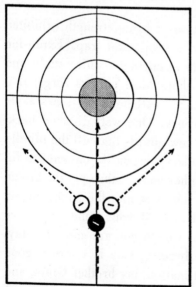

FIG. 76

Splitting two guards and following through.

5. If the guard covers a "shot rock", try to run the guard through onto the shot rock and "split" them both.

6. If two guards are side by side and a stone's width apart, or nearly so, play a follow-through shot. Play to go between these stones. Quite often you will not only remove both guards, but follow through to "lie shot" as well (see Fig. 76).

When two guards lie close together but one ahead of the other (as in Fig. 77), play the corner of the front stone (i.e. the one nearest the player delivering).

FIG. 77

Removing Guards.

Removing two guards but striking the inside corner of the front stone. This will remove your stone as well.

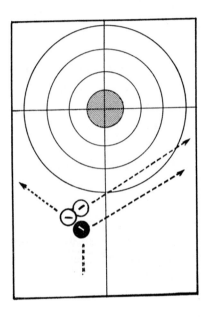

8. When a guard is on the front ring or just in front of the house, play quietly to save your stone so that it will roll to the side rings.

9. When deciding on the amount of ice necessary to remove a guard, keep in mind any advantage there might be in hitting the guard on the left corner or the right corner. Watch the position of your own rocks in the house, or your opponent's, before the shot is played.

10. Do not act too hastily or wait too long before deciding to remove guards. If your opponent has one shot in the house, you need not become panicky, but if a second stone of the opposition finds its way into the rings, act at once whether the scoreboard is for you or against.

Drawing Ports

Drawing a port is often an alternative to removing a guard. Play the port every time if your opponents are lying shot and partially guarded. If you get through the port all well and good, but make certain that if you do not get through, the key guard is removed.

When drawing into the house through a port, be alert for the following:

1. If either of the stones creating the port is a key rock in your planning of the end, be sure to give sufficient ice so as not to disturb it.

2. If both are enemy stones, don't gamble too much if the port is narrow. It would be better to "block" the hole in some cases if it means that you might "open up the end".

3. Play the turn that provides a natural gateway through the port (see Fig. 78).

4. If the two stones forming the opening are close to the house, watch for the "rub". It may give you a much better shot (see Fig. 78).

5. Play a port that allows a stone to curl in toward centre rather than one where the rock is pulling away from centre (see Fig. 78).

6. Do not try to draw through a port into the rings if there is an easier method of doing so.

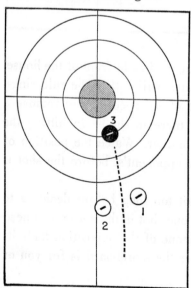

FIG. 78

Drawing a Port

Play the turn that provides a natural gateway. In this case, an out-turn. A rub off No. 1 might help to bury No. 3 more completely.

In this case the out-turn allows the stone to curl in toward the centre of the rings.

7. If a narrow port exists and is formed by at least one of your own stones (the one a little closer to the rings) a raise is usually a much better shot (see Fig. 79).

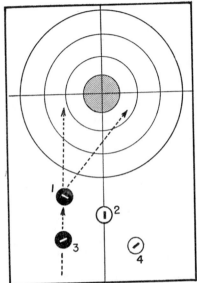

FIG. 79

Drawing a Port

Sometimes it is not advisable to draw the port. In this case a raise is much more practical because you can bury No. 1 behind Nos. 2 and 4 where it cannot be followed, or it could be raised straight away and be guarded by No. 3.

Striking (When to Hit)

For instructional purposes, I am differentiating between "chap and lie" and striking. I will use the term striking to apply in removing a stone with firm weight, i.e. good hack weight. In my opinion, hack weight or striking should be reserved for defensive play only and should be called upon only in cases of emergency. Too many curlers cannot resist the temptation to use this weight on any take-out shot. Younger members, in particular, are guilty of wasting many of their stones by playing too much weight. True there is a lot of thrill to be gained by a crisp hack shot that smacks its target then ricochets off another stone or two, but the average player is not skilful enough as a marksman to be consistent. In keeping a point score during a match, a player receives two points if he strikes and remains in the rings, but only one point if he hits then rolls out of the house. However, here are the exceptions or emergencies when striking is pardonable:

1. On frosty ice, heavily pebbled ice, or dirty ice
2. On swingy or wet ice

3. Removing guards
4. Completing a double take-out
5. Defensive play during the last end when you want to hit opposition rocks and roll out of the rings so they will have no backing

Fast running shots have one use only in the curling game, and that is for the purpose of making a very fine wick with enough force to move a stone the distance desired. A firm hack-weight shot will move two, three, or four rocks as far as they need go, and such a shot, if required, will likely be played more accurately with hack weight by 98% of the curlers.

BUILDING AN END

One of the biggest thrills of my life came as a result of scoring an 8-end in a match that took place at the Amphitheatre Rink in Winnipeg during the 1949 Brier Playoffs. Fred Wilmot, of Douglas, was the unfortunate skip of the rink against whom this crime was perpetrated, and the blame for it should not be laid at the doorstep of Fred and his rink, as they were good curlers; otherwise they would not have reached the final round-robin. Not one of us in our team during that fourth end ever dreamed of its happening, not until Fred went down to play his last stone; then the possibility dawned on us.

It was a very crooked sheet of ice, and up and downhill to boot. My boys were "drawing to a dime" that day, and Fred's men were slipping through the house trying to pass our stones through. The least bit of overweight (even a light hack weight) caused the rocks to back up towards centre, so that as we kept our stones well scattered and left good-sized openings in the centre of the house, there was lots of room to slip through. By the time Fred came to throw his last stone, we had seven rocks in the rings, and when his shot unfortunately struck a guard in front, I had the job of getting the eighth counter "in there". Let me tell you I was as nervous as a "treed cat". My knees were playing a tune that was far from being "A Russian Lullaby", and I think I would have been calmer if the seven stones in the ring had been Wilmot's. How I made the eighth one good, I'll never know.

But the point I want to get at is this: You don't plan to build an eight-end every time you play, but a large end is more probable if you place your rocks properly. If you are interested, Fig. 80 shows the positions of the eight stones at the conclusion of that hectic end. Only one of these had been moved by the Wilmot rink, therefore you may get some idea of positional play in building up an end.

FIG. 80

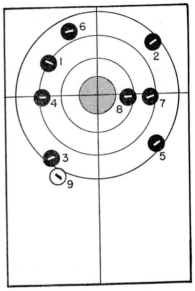

Building an End

Here are the final positions of the stones at the completion of an eight-end score during the Manitoba Brier Playdowns at the Amphitheatre in Winnipeg, in February, 1949.

The eight stones are numbered in the exact order in which they were played by members of the team. No. 9 is Wilmot's last stone which pushed No. 3 up a few inches. It was previously biting the twelve-foot circle. The stones were placed well to the side and in a line with each other as far as possible. This provided a smaller target to shoot at. The centre of the house was kept open until my last rock.

Most skips in building an end have few worries until they get to the point where they have two or three stones in the house, then they wonder where to place the next one. It is comparatively simple to sit down and place the stones theoretically, but you have a horse of a different colour when it comes to the actual reality. Figs. 81 and 82 illustrate the skip's dream of how he would like to have his players place eight stones in the rings, but the actual realization of such a dream requires the opposition missing with their stones and his own players executing flawlessly the shots he calls for, all of which adds up to a page from "Alice in Wonderland".

A more realistic, but much more exasperating, approach to building up an end, supposes the opposition to be in the game, too, and with some say as to how big an end it is going to be. Many good-sized ends materialize with your opponents making most of their shots, too. Fig. 83 illustrates a strategy that often works out successfully.

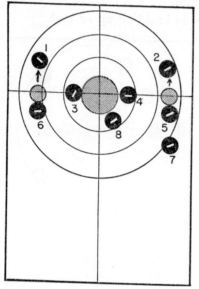

FIG. 81

A Perfect Eight End

Perfect spacing of eight stones (assuming No. 8 is last rock of the end). There is lots of space for opposing stones to slip through the house without disturbing "the dream". Nos. 1 and 2 were originally on the tee line and were raised by Nos. 5 and 6 in perfect line to prevent a double target. No. 7 might have been placed in front of No. 6 or behind No. 3 or 4. The latter is more dangerous for fear of disturbing No. 3 or No. 4 in trying to get to the back rings. By the time No. 4 has been played, the first four stones are in a perfect line with each other to reduce the possibility of double-wicks by the opposition. It is more advantageous to place stones Nos. 5 and 6 in front of Nos. 1 and 2. If these were placed in front of Nos. 3 and 4 the opposing skip would be more tempted to play for the wick, but when placed at the side in front of Nos. 1 and 2 he becomes more cautious and tries to save the end by playing to the stones nearer centre.

In building up an end, it is imperative to keep your stones in front of the opposition's rocks if possible. That is one of the strongest weapons of "Frenchy" D'Amour of Trail, B.C., 1948 Dominion Champion. On keen ice Frenchy is a pastmaster himself at playing just enough weight to move enemy stones back far enough to be out of contention, yet in the rings, where they provide backing for his stones. In my estimation, Frenchy is one of the best individual curlers in Canada to-day. He seldom wastes his own rocks because he prefers draw, or just-over-draw, weight when calling his own shots.

If opposing stones are behind the tee, play enough weight to move them back. Freezing to them is not good strategy unless the

FIG. 82

Another Combination for a Perfect Eight End

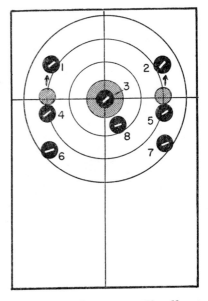

The spacing of the stones is even better here as there were originally only three rocks on the tee line. Nos. 1 and 2 were raised by Nos. 4 and 5. After No. 7 has been placed, the player in the hack at the other end sees only a target of three widely spaced rocks to shoot at. Similarly, after No. 5 shot is completed. The strategy in raising Nos. 1 and 2 is twofold. It leaves room in the front rings for another draw, and even if the opposition plays a double take-out on Nos. 3 and 2, or Nos. 3 and 1, the chances are his stone will roll out of the rings, or remain in the back rings as backing for your other stones in front. Always try to place your stones so that they will maintain the advantage of being in front of enemy rocks after any shot by members of the rival rink.

skip does so, because if you freeze to a stone all the other player has to do is hit your stone quietly and he will be frozen to your rock in turn. Then you have no alternative but to do the same. This will not help you to build an end. Do not allow rocks to "bunch" if you expect to score a big end. Many an end starts out with a draw to the face of a stone in the back rings, and a continual repetition of this develops into a formation like a cluster of grapes. I have seen this happen time and again, and I cannot for the life of me recall having emerged from one of these clusters with a count of more than one or two. Sometimes, in a situation like this, you find that you have last rock but you might as well throw it out the window because, if you play it, you can do nothing but harm. If "bunching" of rocks threatens to develop, draw your next stone to the other side of the house even if your opponent has "shot rock"; that is, if you have last shot that end. Even without the last rock, it is sometimes advisable to change the end around by changing your strategy and waiting for a "break".

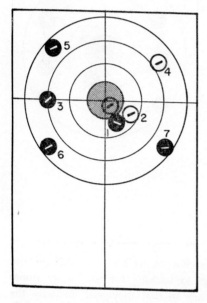

FIG. 83

Playing for a Big End

Here is an example of a more realistic problem. There are three stones to come and you have last rock. No. 1 is frozen, or almost frozen, to No. 2. At first glance it appears as if you should try to push No. 2 out of the rings, which at best is a tricky shot. The following strategy was used by a well-known skip in a bonspiel game. He ignored No. 2 and played a take-out on No. 4. His rival skip then elected to try to draw behind No. 1 for shot rock. As the ice was tricky, he dared not take a chance on "killing" No. 1. As the first skip had foreseen, the attempted draw ended up in a perfect position for a "double" (for a draw almost anywhere in the two foot circle made the "double" possible). The logical play for the unfortunate skip was a guard on the eight foot ring, for third shot, as he was three points up at the time.

Here are a few more ideas to keep in mind when building an end:

1. Play a close guard on any "pockets" that may develop with your stones (see Fig. 84). A smart skip will immediately draw to the front of, or hit into, a pocket of opposing rocks if you fail to protect it.

2. If outside ice (i.e. ice on the side of the sheet) is fairly keen, draw around the outside of "tramp" stones in front of the house, particularly when these "tramps" are about half-way between centre line and the outside edge of the sheet (see Fig. 85).

3. Use rolls to line up your stones (horizontally or vertically) or to keep them well scattered.

4. Play for "nibblers" or "biters" on the twelve-foot ring if the ice suits and your players are adept at the draw. If the sheets of

ice have scantling "dividers", there is often no more than enough room for a stone to "bite" the twelve-foot circle on either side. The target for enemy rocks is thereby reduced considerably because the scantling prevents the opposition from hitting your stone on the outside corner. Charlie Kerr was the best lead man I ever had in this respect. He was uncanny in his ability to "nibble" the outside of the twelve-foot ring. You will find that the "nibblers", scantling or no scantling, are harder to hit than most rocks. I have seen the opposing skip's face get two tints whiter when faced with one of these.

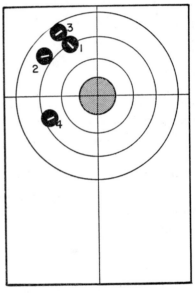

FIG. 84

Protecting a "Pocket"

Either Nos. 1 and 2, or 1, 2, and 3, form a "pocket" which is ruinous to building an end. No. 4, if properly placed, may save some of the bacon. Notice that No. 4 is placed to cover No. 3 which is centred between 1 and 2. If the ice draws well with an out-turn, No. 4 should be slightly closer to centre.

5. Place your stones to take advantage of any backing there might be. Any time your opponent drives one of your stones onto one of his own in the back rings, you are one shot up on him, and, theoretically, if you have last stone, you should score an extra point (see Fig. 86).

6. Use the cover of a long guard to draw your stones into the house and line them up single file in behind the guard. If the guard is removed, replace it. This strategy works well where there is a "run" in the ice that prevents over-draw shots from pulling in far enough to disturb your line. Normally, this strategy may backfire unless your rocks are protected and are lined up almost touching

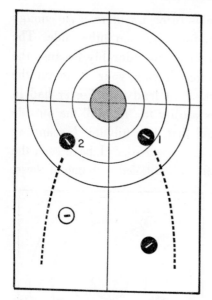

FIG. 85

Drawing Past Guards on the Outside

Try to have Nos. 1 and 2 stop short of the tee line for three reasons:

1. Opposing stones must hit them. They cannot become "shot" by drawing to the face of these stones.

2. If they do hit either of these stones, the chances are they will just move them across but not out of the rings.

3. Both stones would have to be moved at least ten feet to leave the rings. If so, enemy stones would roll out of the house, too. The ice and amount of "pull" must be right to attempt this strategy. If No. 1 were moved to the other side of the rings, draw another into its original position.

each other so that no draw shot can creep in between them.

7. If your opponents are hitting well and seemingly refuse to allow you to build an end, switch the strategy. One game I well remember in a final bonspiel match. Leo Johnson and his rink were hitting everything we put into the house. I had been playing the out-turn side of the ice which "swung" more than the in-turn side. This didn't bother the Johnson rink. They were smacking everything on the nose. So I switched to the in-turn side where the ice ran straight, and the first thing I knew they missed a few and we scored a big "six". It was a different story from then on.

A change in strategy can take other forms.

    1. Change to drawing to the centre first instead of to the side.

    2. Change to raising short guards.

    3. Change to drawing behind guards.

    4. Start mixing up your stones with your opponent's.

    5. Draw to the front rings instead of the tee line.

The best way to score a big end is to keep playing for it. A five end is worth five singles. My practice has always been to try to score

FIG. 86

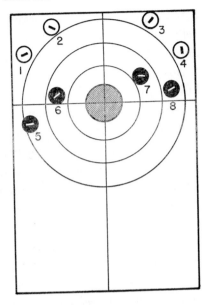

Taking Advantage of Backing

Stones Nos. 1, 2, 3, and 4 all have excellent possibilities of backing for any stone immediately in front. They also provide a good barrier if a stone is chipped sideways. For instance, No. 4 is possible backing for No. 7 as well as No. 8, and the same applies with No. 2. Either Nos. 5 or 6 could strike Nos. 1 or 2 and remain on the rings. When asking your player for a draw, be alert to the possible use of backing. The exception occurs if it causes "bunching" with stones already in the rings.

one good-sized end no later than half-way through the match. This provides breathing space. But it would be foolhardy to concentrate solely on big ends. Take your ones and twos where you get them. Don't play against the law of averages and gamble for an end where the odds are badly against you. This is a definite mandate during the last few ends of a game. Take your fours, fives, and sixes where they come naturally, but don't try to stretch a one into a three, or a two into a five, or you will turn victory into defeat so quickly that you won't know what hit you.

When your opponent gives you your chance to chalk up a real end by a few ill-timed misses and all that remains for you is to remove a stone to achieve it, don't get over-anxious. Play your normal take-out weight; concentrate on swinging at the broom in your usual unhurried style; take a deep breath while you are in the hack, and say to yourself: "Look at that broom, Jonesy! Look at that broom!"

STRATEGY DURING THE FINAL ENDS

The "pressure ends" in a curling match are the last three ends. Here is where experience and coolness count as well as the use of every bit of strategic knowledge a skip possesses. Unlike many fast action sports, such as hockey, football, and baseball, where the reflexes must work fast and almost instinctively, curling is a deliberate game where team play is the function, but individual performance is the essence, inasmuch as the time lapse betwen shots builds up a terrific nervous and mental tension in each player. As shot follows shot, with each mounting in importance, as two evenly matched teams move closer to the last and most dramatic end, the pressure increases to a point that defies description.

It is during these ends that many rinks or players "crack". The tension becomes so great that many a curler loses his nerve, and with it the smooth, effortless delivery that characterized him earlier in the game. The skip loses his confidence and the cleverness of his strategy somehow disappears. The cool daring of his decisions melts into irresolution and uncertainty. The infection is contagious to his team, and soon all, by their actions and facial expressions, register resignation and acceptance of the bitter pill of defeat.

Time and time again I have seen this drama re-enacted and each time on a different stage and by different players. Sometimes the cause is inexperience, or stage-fright; sometimes it is pure funk from lack of self-confidence, but more often it results from unsound judgment on the part of the skip in the use of his strategy.

Knowledge begets confidence, and confidence breeds power. When a skip profits from experience, he will have the knowledge he needs to direct the play of the final ends. The rest will follow in due order. Experience is a great teacher, and a large part of the knowledge of strategy that I have gained in competitive play, I owe to the curlers at the Strathcona Curling Club of Winnipeg, where the standard of play was of high calibre.

Among the thousands of Curling Clubs in Canada, the Strathcona Club holds seven Canadian Championships out of twenty played (to 1949) and twelve provincial titles out of twenty-three competed for. I am not using these pages to praise my home club, rather to explain why, when we played two nights a week for many years against such redoubtable skips as Gordon Hudson, Leo Johnson, Bob Gourlay, Ross Kennedy, Al Wakefield, Ness Wise, Cliff Wise, and others, I gained a tremendous amount of experience in the use of strategy in skipping, and particularly so during the last three ("pressure") ends of the games, most of which were thirteen-end or "last rock" twelve-end battles. Each game was played for everything that was in it, just as if we were playing for the Brier Tankard. Rivalry was very keen, and every point made was considered a strategic victory. The last three ends of each and every one of these tests of team strength was followed closely by a small gallery of onlookers who were always on hand to enjoy the battle of wits that went on between skips, who as early as the ninth end began jockeying for position so as to have the advantage on the last end.

Several winters of this strenuous competition toughened us for bonspiel play so that a hectic point-for-point struggle with an opponent became just another club game, and even with the roars of five thousand spectators added for good measure, the spectacle only accelerated the pulse rate a few beats. It failed to unsettle the mental equilibrium that constant exposure to competitive play develops in a player or a team.

When considering the strategy to be employed during the final ends, the score of the game is the determining factor. In order to reduce the possibility of repetition to a minimum, yet at the same time cover adequately the variety of situations that a skip is often confronted with, I shall attempt to deal with each of the last three ends, as well as a possible extra end, from three viewpoints: (All references are to a twelve-end game. In a ten-end game, the eighth, ninth, and tenth ends would be the final ends.)

1. Assuming the score is three or more points in your favour.

2. Assuming the score is against you by three or more points.

3. Assuming the score is very close, with not more than two points difference.

Tenth-End Strategy

1. *When you are three or more points up*

Let us assume that you have just completed the ninth end in a twelve-end match, and that you have the advantage of last rock in playing the tenth. Your chief concern is to protect your points lead and prevent any panic from creeping into your play or your strategy. Do not change your style of play unless your opponent changes his.

Carry on as if you were playing the fourth end instead of the tenth, but be alert. With a three or more point advantage and with last stone, your sole aim is to score on this end to maintain your advantage. If you do, your opponent may score one, two, or even three on the eleventh end, and you will still have last rock on the twelfth with no worse than being one point up "coming home." Try to play the tenth end as follows:

(a) If the opposing skip places the first stone in front of the rings, remove it. Do not allow your players to use excessive weight. Keep the front of the house clear and open.

(b) If by chance you strike opposing stones and replace them with your own, or if your player fails to remove an opposition rock and they draw a stone into the rings behind it, again play to remove the front stone. In "giving ice" to your player for this shot, take a look to see if a corner of the "buried" rock is exposed. If so, use the turn on the exposed side so that if your player misses the front stone he may strike the corner of the stone in the rings instead (see Fig. 87).

(c) Assuming that the other skip does not elect to draw behind the guard, but asks for a draw to the side of the rings instead, remove

FIG. 87

When removing a guard on the tenth end use the out-turn in a case like this, where the corner of No. 1 is exposed. Play close enough to make certain of removing either No. 1 or No. 2. If the out-turn falls away, use the in-turn on the other side. Should your player fail to remove No. 1 or No. 2, and your opposition places No. 3 in the rings, play to remove No. 3.
Should your player remove No. 2 in the first instance, then No. 3 is placed in the rings, play the correct ice to strike No. 1 on the inside corner for a possible wick and double take-out.

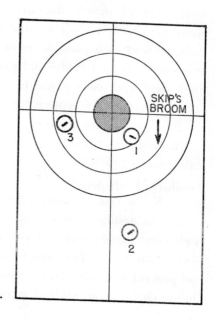

the stone in the rings. Do not bother with the guard in any situation of this kind, where a single enemy rock is exposed (see Fig. 87).

(d) As long as opposing stones are protected by guards, keep playing to remove these guards (with exceptions illustrated in Fig. 88). Remember you are three or more points ahead, and as long as the front of the house is fairly open, keep hitting any exposed rocks of the rival team. Do not worry too much about a single stone in front of the rings, until you get a chance to remove it, or are forced to do so because of enemy stones behind it. A situation like the one illustrated in Fig. 88 often occurs during the tenth end and requires care in the selection of the right shot.

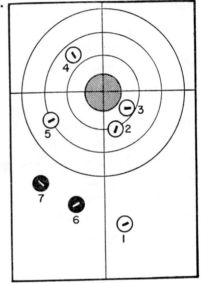

FIG. 88

Even when three points up, this situation calls for care. Your opponents lie four, and if they score even two or three, they will gain the advantage, so there is little to be gained by trying to cut their score down by hitting stones Nos. 4 and 5, which are exposed. No. 2 is the key enemy stone and should be the object of your attack. If Nos. 2 and 3 were perfectly "buried" behind No. 1, then No. 1 would have to be removed, so that you would have a reasonable chance to use your last rock to score. What would you do if this was the situation when you came to play your last rock on the tenth end? (Answer—in-turn draw between Nos. 6 and 7.)

(e) If you get into trouble in the tenth end, play the percentage shots or those where you have two or three chances of getting a roll, wick, rub, or raise. But above all give yourself, as skip, a chance with your last rock. Even if your own rocks are in front of the house blocking the way, don't try to raise them into the rings or you will be playing into the opposition's hands. Get them out of the way and make certain that no lucky "breaks" can occur against you. You should not be gambling when the score is in your favour.

(f) Do not try to draw behind opposition guards unless you have to do so with your last two stones.

(g) Use hack-weight, not runner-weight, in removing stones from the rings or in front of the rings.

(h) If there are no problems about enemy stones in front of the rings, play the tenth end as you would any other end where you have last rock.

(i) If your opposition has several stones in the house when you play your last rock, cut down your weight to draw, or no more than over-tee weight if you have backing. It is important to score on the tenth end.

(j) Without last stone on the tenth and three or more points up, try to score one if possible to retain the offensive, but you cannot afford to concentrate too much on keeping the "front" of the house open.

Draw your first stone of the end into the rings and try to play as you would any normal end. Your object is to take the offensive and keep your opponents hitting, then if you get a chance to guard the key rock, do so with a close guard. This will make it difficult to score against you.

Many skips try to play a defensive end under such circumstances and place the first rock in front of the rings, but too many times things go wrong and the opposition scores a big end to put them back in the game. Keep the end open and carry the play to the enemy, then take advantage of his misses to close up the end in the later stages. Draw to the side rings first, then if you get to the point where you have one stone on either side, draw one to the centre. That is the one to place a close guard on if you get the chance.

2. *When you are three or more points down*

Let us put the shoe on the other foot while playing the tenth. You have last rock but the score is decidedly against you. However, if you can come within one point of tying the score you will be back in contention again; in fact, you will gain somewhat of an advantage, for you can still allow one point on the eleventh, and be only two down coming home with last rock in your favour. Personally, I have never become disconsolate in a hard-fought match to find myself in such a position. It has many advantages.

(a) If your opponents play the first stone in front of the rings, draw in behind (in front of the tee-line). They will likely waste a stone trying to get at yours; if so, draw another to the side rings. You will have to use a little daring on this end because you will want to score at least two (if you are three down).

(b) If your opponents draw into the rings and behind the tee-line, try to draw to the face of their stone and push it back a foot or so. A freeze shot sometimes invites "bunching" of rocks and does not produce many big ends (see Fig. 89).

(c) Play very quiet weight for most shots as you want to save your stones and keep them in the rings. (Refer to the section on "How to Build a Big End" pp. 124-131).

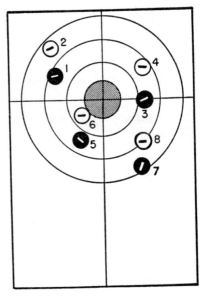

FIG. 89

If you are three or four points in arrears playing the last few ends, place your stones in front of your opponent's. The more effective your opposition is at hitting, the closer your stones should be to their backing.

Stones in diagram Fig. 89 have been numbered in pairs and show four situations of increased severity. No. 1 is placed in front of No. 2 in a normal situation at the beginning of the tenth end, and similarly No. 3 in front of No. 4; but if the opposition is hitting well and not leaving many of your rocks in the house, it is even necessary to draw to the front of enemy stones, like No. 6 and No. 8, in the hope that you might get a chance to raise them later. The position of No. 7 in front of No. 8 represents a last desperate attempt to score two or more. Each pair of stones in the diagram represents a separate problem, each at a different stage during the playing of the end.

(d) Get as many of the first five of your stones into the rings as possible. Use the last three to try to engineer the big end.

(e) If three points down, do not become greedy and gamble for four or five when two or three are certain. This is the crucial end where the law of averages must be given first consideration.

(f) Take any points you can get on the tenth end, rather than give your opponent one, in the hope that you can score a big end on the eleventh.

3. When the score is close

The closer the game, when playing the tenth end, the more necessary it is to score. If you have last rock, keep the end open to make it as simple as possible for you to effect your last shot. Every stone you ask your team to play is directed toward that one objective. Play for a big end if possible but make certain that you score at least one point.

(a) Remove any guard in front of the rings. If these guards are well to the side, it is not necessary, but a clear space of three or four feet on each side of the centre line should be kept open.

(b) If your opponents draw to the back rings, play enough weight to pass them back and out of the circles. If they draw to the front rings, play enough weight for a roll to either side. If they

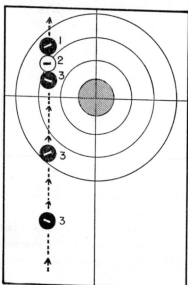

FIG. 90

In a case where opponent has played a "freeze" (No. 2) to your stone (No. 1) behind the tee-line, strike No. 2 with No. 3. You will sacrifice No. 1 but No. 3 will remain frozen in front of No. 2.

If such a freeze is located in front of the tee, play sufficient weight to remove both No. 1 and No. 2.

freeze to your stones behind the tee-line, play quiet take-out weight. Sacrifice the rock that they froze to and leave your own in front of theirs (see Fig. 90). If they freeze to any of your stones in front of the tee, play a good hack-weight and remove both stones. However, if they freeze to one of your rocks in a situation such as the one shown in Fig. 91, guard the raise.

FIG. 91

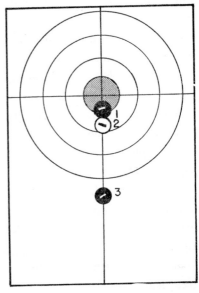

Where there are only three or four stones to be played in the tenth end of a close game, and your opponent freezes or draws very close to your "shot" rock, you have no alternative but to guard his possible raise. You can gain no advantage by trying to move No. 2. Then if the opposing skip fails to improve the situation, you may attempt to draw for two points.

(c) When placing your draws in the rings, try to keep your stones just in front of the tee line so that your opponents have to move them back to lie shot. The only exception occurs when you are forced to play for position when you have other stones in the rings.

(d) In a low-scoring match where both teams are playing well and the opposing skip is very accurate with his draw weight, avoid getting too many rocks in the rings where pockets, to which he can draw, can be formed. If there is any such danger imminent, draw to the back rings well away from your other rocks.

(e) When you have last stone, any guards that you may play to protect the key rock should be within a foot or two of the shot you are trying to protect.

(f) With last rock against you, have your lead place his first stone in front of the rings so that you can use it for cover later, and as often as your opposing skip removes this stone, replace it with another. This can go on until the guard is struck "dead on" or full, leaving the opposition rock in its place. Now use this stone for protection and ask for a draw behind it.

(g) In a tie game, it is almost imperative that you score on the tenth. Without the advantage of last rock you may have to take chances. Look for any cover you can find for your stones. Play raises or draws in behind. Keep your rocks in front, if possible, and wait for a break that will allow you to "bury" one of your stones.

Whether the score is even, whether one or two points separate you, or whether you have last stone or not, there is only one thing to remember. You must score at least one on the tenth end if you are to keep the offensive. Every play, every shot, and every bit of strategy put to use must be directed with that in mind.

Eleventh-End Strategy

Oddly enough the eleventh end is the "eleventh hour" for many a team. What appears to be a match well in hand, for no apparent reason suddenly becomes life's darkest hour. The eleventh end is no nightmare to a steady, experienced rink whose personnel have weathered the storm on other numerous occasions. Experience is a great teacher and we must learn by doing and by understanding why and where mistakes have been made. One of my greatest strategical errors was made as a young skip during the eleventh end of a match in the Tucker Competition, which was originally the emblem of the City of Winnipeg Curling Championship. With our original "kid rink" we had reached the "eights" of the event and were drawn to play the veteran Jack Campbell and his Granite Club team, composed of Bill Noble, Harry Mawhinney and another whom I cannot recall. At the end of the tenth end we were two points up, and then the fatal eleventh reared up at us. My first error was to ask Ted Linklater, our lead, to place his stone in front of the house. Jack Campbell daringly had his lead Mawhinney draw into the rings behind it. Then the fun began. Instead of immediately removing our front stone, or trying to raise it on to the shot rock, I asked Linklater to try to chip out the shot stone (one of the most difficult shots in curling).

This was my second "faux pas". He missed, and Campbell drew another stone in behind. I tried to have the second man, Dave Turnbull save the day, but he was short in his attempt to draw behind the guard. By this time, the damage had been done and, try as we might to clear a pathway into the rings, our opposition had us on the run and played their shots flawlessly to prevent us from making a recovery. When Bill Noble, their third man, walked to the score-board at the completion of the end, he marked up four points. We failed to make up the two point deficit on the twelfth and final end. The four of us were a pretty humble crew when we walked off the ice. I had literally thrown away the game on the eleventh end, when we had a reasonably safe margin, by complacent and slovenly thinking in planning the skipping strategy.

1. *When you are three or more points up*

Should you have scored on the tenth and assumed a lead of three points or more, even though the opposing skip has last rock on the eleventh end, play it the same way as described for the tenth end where you were playing under similar circumstance. For emphasis, let me repeat briefly the most important points to remember:

(a) Play the first stone into the rings.

(b) Keep the front open with hack-weight shots.

(c) Build up an end with quiet take-out shots and draws, if given a chance.

(d) Remove opposing rocks if they are in the house or close to the front rings where there is any danger of their being raised.

(e) Take the initiative if given the opportunity, but do not allow your opponents any chance to engineer a score of two or more points.

(f) Should you be lying shot, with your opponents second, play to remove their stone as long as it is as easy to hit as it is to draw for second shot (see Fig. 92).

(g) If you lie two shots, and third shot is against you, draw for third shot (see Fig. 93).

(h) Assuming your opponent has last rock, try to prevent him from blanking the end which is good strategy for him if he cannot score more than one. This is one very good reason why Fig. 93, below, illustrates the necessity of having two shot stones. The end cannot be blanked.

(i) If your opponent manages to protect a shot rock, play to remove his second shot if it is accessible, and if he has two or more

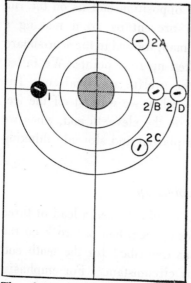

FIG. 92

No. 1 is your shot stone. No. 2, A, B, C and D represent four different positions of an opposing second shot. Each position is attacked in a different manner:

2A—Remove with quiet take-out weight or back-ring weight.

2B—Remove with quiet take-out weight and if possible remain in the same position.

2C—Play light-hack weight and roll to right side or centre.

2D—Draw along side to the face of a stone in this position unless a run in the ice makes it easy to hit.

The object of the strategy in each of the above cases, is to lie two shots, which would not be the case if you hit an opposing stone and rolled out.

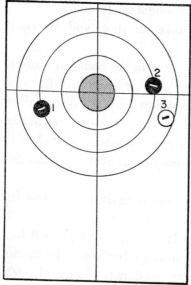

FIG. 93

In a case where you lie two (Nos. 1 and 2) with third shot against you, there is no advantage in trying to remove No. 3. Play a draw to the centre instead.

A little bad luck could drive No. 3 on to No. 2 and change the whole complexion of the end, if you tried to hit.

shots in the rings, always play to hit the one closest to the front. Thus you have a chance for a roll or a double take-out.

If you have last stone on this end, play it the same way, although it is not advisable to blank the end in order to have last rock coming home. Take your points here if you can. Four or more up coming home should be a safe margin. Should you have three or four shots against you when you play your last stone, play it quietly and make certain you count one. Play the safest shot where the least chance of slip exists. Resist the temptation to blast enemy stones out of the house with a runner to cut the "end" down. If you miss, or hit and roll out, you will upset your team mates for the final end.

2. *When you are three or more points down*

Whereas the emphasis is on defensive play when you enjoy a fair margin of points playing the eleventh end, the reverse is the case if you find yourself in arrears at this stage of the game. Offensive tactics with daring strategy are inevitable if you are to score sufficient points to be a contender again. Draw, or no more than back-ring, weight is necessary to keep your rocks in play. Only when your third man, or you as skip, play can you afford the luxury of over-weight shots, and then only for the purpose of changing the positions of the stones in the rings to alter the complexion of the end.

There is no specific strategy to be employed here other than that described for similar score conditions in the tenth end, or in the section under the heading "How to Build an End". Watch the strategy of your rival skip and if he shows too much desire for defensive play, take advantage of it by placing a stone: (a) On any "run" in the rings where it is difficult to hit; (b) "Biting" the outside edge of the twelve-foot circle; (c) In the back rings. (The farther back a stone is, the more distant the target, and the greater the chance of a miss.)

Try to entice the opposition to draw by placing your first stone well back in the rings. Do not attempt to remove opposition rocks until your third man plays. Draw in front of them and wait for a break or a miss or two before raising your stones onto theirs. If necessary, leave their shot stone alone for a while and concentrate on getting second and third shot, then use a later opportunity to remove it.

You will often have to gamble on this end, but do not go overboard in taking chances. If you can come within one or two points of tying the match, you will still have a fair chance on the twelfth end.

3. *When the score is close*

The closer the score, the stronger the argument that it is good strategy to try to blank the end if you have last rock. This is even more evident if it is a low-scoring match (e.g. 5-4 or 6-5 or 7-6). Such a score usually indicates that the skip in each case has been making his last rock count. Therefore, great importance has been attached to last stone in each and every end. If the opposing skip has been playing well, you will have all the more reason to respect his ability and the importance of his last rock. But preconceived strategy for blanking the eleventh in a game where erratic curling in previous ends had created a high score (e.g. 13-11, 14-13, or even 10-10) would not be good judgment. If the progress of the end indicates a change in the scoring pattern so that there is no more than one or two stones in the rings when the skip plays his first shot, there would be some justification for purposely trying to blank the

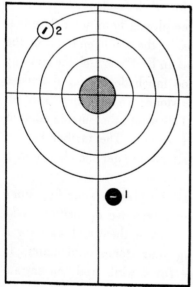

FIG. 94

Blanking this end would be pardonable if you were one or two points up. By removing No. 2 and rolling out yourself, you would carry last rock into the twelfth with no change in score.

There might be a temptation to try to wick No. 1 into the rings along with your own rock, but the odds are against counting any more than one. Even if you were two up, I would still blank the end.

There would be no point in blanking the end if No. 2 were your stone. By all means try to wick in No. 1 with your own to score three.

end. Do not let this become an obsession. One shot can rule out this strategy quickly.

Figures 94 and 95 illustrate two situations where in one case a blank end is justifiable, but in the other it would be poor strategy. (In both cases, we will assume that you are one or two points up.)

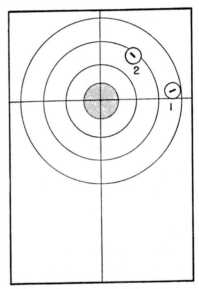

FIG. 95

With two stones against you in the positions of No. 1 and No. 2, your chances of blanking the end are small. Play a quiet draw with No. 2 as backing and take your one point, particularly if it will give you a three point lead for the twelfth.

There is one exception. If the ice is tricky and your team has been erratic in hitting during the game, you might try the shot, provided it were a tie game or you were one point up.

4. When to Blank the Eleventh End

There are many combinations or rock positions possible in the eleventh end where you may be faced with the problem of whether or not it is wise to try to blank the end with your last shot. In each and every case your decision should be based on two qualifying factors:

(a) The existing score

(b) The importance of having last rock in the twelfth end

Personally, I prefer having last stone on the twelfth end unless we are three or more points up. I would rather be two down coming home with last rock in my favour, than tie, or one up, coming home without the advantage of last stone. In a very close game the best strategical position is a one or more point advantage with the use of last rock. Therefore, when you are studying your last shot on the eleventh, keep this in mind.

Twelfth-End Strategy

In curling, there are no thrills comparable to those experienced during the twelfth end of a match that has been close and hard-fought throughout. And if the game in question is the finale of a long series of matches in bonspiel play, climaxing a week or two of continuous curling, the tension built up in players and spectators alike is unbelievable. The fortunes of days of exhausting efforts, sweeping and delivering rock after rock, hang by a slender thread on the strategy and play of a single end. At this point, one error in judgment of weight or ice or sweeping by player or skip, can never be redeemed. It is too late to make a mistake.

The greatest thrill of my curling days occurred during the twelfth and thirteenth ends of a game against Ab Gowanlock of Glenboro in the final match of the Brier Playdowns in 1936. The winner was to represent Manitoba in the Canadian Finals at Toronto. The match was played before fifteen hundred spectators at the Ampitheatre in Winnipeg. By the time we had reached the twelfth end in this hectic see-saw contest, the spectators were keyed up to a point of nervous exhaustion. Ab and I were both curling steadily that night and the fate of every end had hinged on last rock.

We had scored one on the eleventh to be two up coming home, consequently Ab had the advantage of last stone. I never had considered this an enviable position to be in but, as we had had no opportunity to blank the eleventh end, I called my team (brother Grant, Marv Macintyre, and Charlie Kerr) into a huddle before starting the twelfth end. We decided to play the end open, that is to play the first stone through the house and play rock for rock from then on. Our strategy was based on these arguments: (1) The ice surface was good and it was reasonably easy to hit a rock wherever it might stop in the rings. (2) Even should we miss one shot, Ab could at best count two and we would have last rock playing the extra end. (3) By playing an open end there was less likelihood of the opposition using the cover of guards or the backing of our stones. (4) This was our twenty-fifth, and last, game of the bonspiel, and even though we were dead-tired, we could not afford to give the Gowanlock rink a chance to win on the twelfth.

Charlie Kerr put his first rock through the house as directed. Tom McKnight, Ab's lead, drew to the rings, then Charlie missed his take-out. It looked as if our strategy might backfire. The crowd, sensing the drama in the situation, was hushed and silent between shots, but with every stone delivered thereafter the roars could be heard blocks away. As for me, I hardly recall all the details. I was so tensed that I was in a trance. All I remember is that from the time of Charlie's miss both teams played every stone perfectly and Gowanlock scored two to send the game into overtime.

The thirteenth end was a veritable nightmare. The spectators worked themselves into a wild frenzy as one shot followed another. Ab and his team had conferred and decided to close the end. Their first stone was placed out in front, and when Kerr failed to remove it, they drew another into the rings behind it. A further miss by Charlie and one by Macintyre left Gowanlock with two in the rings, covered by two guards in front, a pretty dismal situation. Grant kept pounding at the guards while Bung Cartmell, Ab's third, and Ab with his first stone replaced them. Ab had one stone left and I had two when I studied the situation. His stone, which was just back of the four-foot ring, was well guarded against a take-out. There were only two alternatives: (1) To remove the guard (in which case, he would replace it); or (2) To draw around it to the face of his shot rock. I made up my mind in a hurry. There was only one choice as far as I was concerned and that was a draw, because I felt I had two chances. But it was necessary to make certain I knew what the feel of perfect weight was if I had to play a dead draw with my last stone. Should I remove the guard, he would replace it and I would be forced to draw to the four-foot circle to win. All I recall is that I was in a daze as I sat in the hack ready to deliver. It was a wide sweeping out-turn draw to the tee-line, directly in front of the shot stone, that resulted. How I got there I don't know. Ab's attempt to follow me was a little narrow and he "rubbed" the guard. The rest was anti-climax, but the excitement of those last two ends will live in my memory forever.

My only purpose in recounting the story is to call attention to the need of consulting all the members of your team in making a decision regarding the strategy to be used in either the twelfth or thirteenth ends. Both are final ends, and the outcome hinges on the play of each member.

1. *When you are three or more points up*

There are a very few points of difference between playing the twelfth end, under such circumstances, and the tenth or eleventh ends.

(a) Play your first stone through the rings so as to provide no backing or cover for opponents' stones. In several curling areas these tactics are frowned on and considered poor sportsmanship and not in harmony with the true spirit of the game. In the Western style of play, it is common practice and brings no reflection on the gentlemanly qualities of a skip. I can understand that wherever the draw game is practised exclusively, such strategy would not meet with the approval of some curlers, but where the more aggressive type of knock-out game is followed, its adherents have fully recognized the importance of this defensive measure.

Bob Gourlay of the Strathcona Club forcibly demonstrated the value of this strategy to me during the twelfth end of a final match in the Purity Flour Competition in the Manitoba 'Spiel in 1936. After a previous game I had cautioned Charlie Kerr, our lead, about using too much energy in tossing his first rock through the house when I signalled such a shot. I suggested that he be more subtle about it and just use enough weight to pass through the rings quietly. Well, we were three up on Bob Gourlay. He had last rock coming home, so I signalled my well-briefed lead to put his stone through. Charlie had listened to my instructions too well. His stone was very quiet and although I swept like mad I could not get it out of the rings. It stopped defiantly just biting the back ring. Gourlay promptly called on Rae Stewart, who in my estimation, was the best lead man to toss a curling rock, to play a freeze to Charlie's stone. Rae did just what he was asked for, and what should have been a comparatively safe margin playing the last end, disappeared so fast we didn't know what had struck us. R. J. Gourlay tied the game. I still remember my words to Charlie Kerr after the match. I said,

"Kerr! Forget that subtle business and throw them into the waiting room if you like, but get them through the house."

(b) Play more weight in removing stones from the rings or from in front of the rings. Try to make certain your stones roll out of the rings, too.

(c) Play any stone through the house if your opponents have no rocks for you to remove.

(d) One point is as good as a million on the last end. If you are three up, all you have to do is make certain your opposition scores no more than two. Play to remove second or third shots.

(e) If any of your own rocks stop in the rings or in front, remove them if you get a chance. They are no good to you unless your opponents have counters in the house, too.

2. When you are three or more points down

Refer to the discussions under the same heading dealing with the tenth or eleventh ends, pp. 136 and 143.

3. When the score is close

There are so many individual situations that might arise during the play of the final end of a match that it is impossible to think of covering all of them in this section. The major strategic problems have been fairly well reviewed elsewhere in these pages, even to the risk of repetition, but as the importance of reducing the number of errors committed by the skip cannot be over-estimated, here are some further observations that I have learned through the bitter experience of having played in many thousand final ends.

Strategy will vary, and is best considered from two angles:

(1) Who has last rock?
(2) What is the score?

Ten different situations can exist. You may have last rock and the score reads 2 up; 1 up; tie; 1 down; 2 down; or your opponent has last rock with similar varieties in score. I'll break this down into two main categories that are created by the use of last rock.

SITUATION 1—LAST ROCK, YOURS—SCORE, 2 UP

Under normal conditions use the same strategy as employed

when three or more up. If the ice is very tricky for hitting, get your first stone into the rings and try to keep it just in front of the tee-line.

SITUATION 2—LAST ROCK, YOURS—SCORE, 1 UP

On normal ice keep the front, and the house, clear. If this situation exists when your lead plays his first stone, signal him to put it through. If the ice is swingy, wet, or very tricky, draw into the house. On this end a skip has only one problem, to make sure that he has no worse than a simple draw or take-out to make with his last rock. If your opponent has only one shot stone, when you play your last, you can afford to hit and roll out of the rings.

Sometimes a situation exists that you cannot improve on. In that case do not play your stone, or if asked to do so, make certain it is short of the hog or over the side-line or scantling. Let well enough alone, is a good motto.

SITUATION 3—LAST ROCK, YOURS—SCORE, TIE

You have no alternative but to score when you find yourself in this position. Keep the front open, and try to place any stones you draw into the rings on, or just in front of, the tee-line. The skip should avoid playing a "runner" himself, if at all possible, as he may have to make a good draw with his last stone.

On some sheets of ice, the in-turn may work much better for a draw than the out-turn. Be sure to keep the in-turn side of the ice open for that final draw if it is needed.

If, when you have to make that final draw, there are two or three opposing stones behind the tee as backing, take ice that will give you the advantage of resting on these stones, but concentrate on tee-line draw weight. Forget the backing once you get into the hack or you will likely be a little heavy and rub an opposing stone, thus losing your shot. Do not have two shots in your mind when playing this final stone of the game. Decide which one you are going to play, and play it.

SITUATION 4—LAST ROCK, YOURS—SCORE, 1 DOWN

This is a favourable position. Theoretically, if your team make all shots and the opponents miss one, you should score two, sufficient to win.

If your opponent places his first stone well in front of the rings, ignore it and draw to the side of the house.

If his first stone is close to the twelve-foot circle, remove it, and try to roll into the rings. Do not allow short guards to remain.

Do not guard at any time during this end unless you use a very short guard in the rings to protect a pocket or when you, as skip, play your first stone to cover a key rock. There are exceptions to every rule, but this is one of the ten commandments in curling. I have seen the opposition wick-in off rocks at the side to lie perfectly buried behind one of our stones. The element of luck enters all curling games, but when you get to the last end you should take every precaution to eliminate the chances of a lucky shot. You can seldom recover from such a "break" at this stage of the game.

Situation 5—Last rock, yours—Score, 2 down

Use the same procedure as you would if you were three down, but do not take quite as many chances. You must score two to stay in the game, so play for two first then try to get the third if possible. Do not allow the front of the house to clog too much; you must have a chance to use your last stone. Theoretically, your opposition has only to miss twice to allow you to score three.

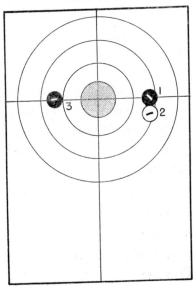

FIG. 96

Do not worry about an enemy stone freezing to your shot rock in the twelfth end. As long as you are shot, draw another stone to the other side of the house for second (No. 3).

If No. 2 were shot, you would have no alternative but to hit it and sacrifice No. 1. This would leave your stone frozen to No. 2 if played properly.

SITUATION 6—LAST ROCK, OPPONENT'S—SCORE, 2 UP

If your team is confident of hitting any stone anywhere, signal your lead to put his stone through. Otherwise draw to the side rings but on the tee-line or in front so that an opposing rock will not be

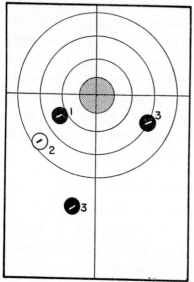

FIG. 97

In the twelfth end of a game in the Brier, I committed the blunder of trying to guard No. 1 with No. 3 instead of playing a draw with No. 3 to the other side of the house.

No. 3 was only a partial guard and Ramsay, the opposing skip, played a beautiful shot to replace No. 1. We were one up at the time without last rock. This error cost us the game.

shot if "frozen" to the face of it. Ignore a "freeze" by your opponents as long as your stone is shot. Draw to the other side of the rings for second shot (see Fig. 96).

Avoid the common error of guarding the shot rock when you have one in the rings. Draw for a second. Second shot is still the best guard in the world. Alf Ramsay of Civic Caledonian Club, Winnipeg, put us out of the Brier in 1948 when I made that same mistake on the twelfth end. Fig. 97 illustrates the position of the rocks involved in the play. We were one up coming home at the time, but the same strategy would have prevailed if we had been two up with last rock against us.

SITUATION 7—LAST ROCK, OPPONENT'S—SCORE, 1 UP

Offensive play is even more necessary when you are a single point up and the rival skip has the decided advantage of last rock. Place your first stone out in front unless the opposition are poor hitters. Play the end to count one, but if you find yourself eventually in the position illustrated in Fig. 96 play for an extra end by drawing for two.

Should the rings be empty when you play your last rock, there are several places to consider putting it:

1. Biting the front ring on the centre line so that they cannot get shot by hitting it
2. On a tricky "run" in the rings
3. On the "button" where it must be moved to score
4. On the four-foot circle in front of the tee-line where a draw cannot pass it easily or where it must be moved back in order to get shot

If your opposition lies one shot when you play your final rock, try to remove it quietly and stay in the rings yourself. Make it necessary for the other skip to play as difficult a shot as possible in order to tie the game.

SITUATION 8—LAST ROCK, OPPONENT'S—SCORE, EVEN

One point is as good as a dozen here. Ignore the number of opposition stones in the rings and concentrate on getting one rock "salted" away. If you do get shot rock, keep guarding it with every bit of granite you have at your disposal. "Bury it so deep that three men, two boys, and a crowbar couldn't get it out of there", to quote Shel Macnicol, an effervescent friend of mine, and known to thousands in the West for his earthy expressions.

Play your first stone in front and keep playing all but the last of them there until you get the protection of one of yours, or one of the opposition's to crawl in behind. I remember a final game in the Grand Challenge many years ago where we played seven of our eight rocks in front of the house before Tommy Thompson finally hit my first stone on the "nose" and I used our eighth stone to draw behind his. That stone won the game when Tommy missed it with his last rock on the twelfth end.

Do not try to make your last rock too good if everything depends on you to get that one shot necessary to win. Too many skips give their opposing skips too much credit in their own minds. No skip, ro matter what his reputation, is super-human. He will often miss a shot that does not appear too difficult. Many times I have made the mistake of being too cautious in a position like this. Instead of passing the shot rock back quietly, I have tried to move it a foot or two if it were on the tee-line so that my rock would have backing. In most cases I was so afraid of pushing the rock too far back that I was short and the rival skip didn't even have to play his last stone. Whatever happens, see to it that your opposing skip has to play his last shot to win.

Situation 9—Last rock, opponent's—Score, 1 down

Use the same strategy as in Situation 8. Play for the tying counter first, then worry about the winning stone. Use no more than the first three or four stones in front of the house. If by that time you have no success, play for the side ice and a miss or two by the opposition.

If you manage to get shot on the four-foot circle or closer, play a close guard with your last stone. Encourage the opponents to hit if necessary. They will be inclined to play over-weight and there is more chance of missing.

Line up your stones along, or close to, the centre line behind a long guard if possible. In this fashion they present a narrow target and discourage a draw from disturbing them as well.

Situation 10—Last rock, opponent's—Score, 2 down

Play for the rings immediately. Leave the guards until you have enough stones in the rings. Take advantage of any raise, guard, wick, or chip. Mix up your stones with your opponent's. Employ the same tactics as if you were three or more down, but if given the opportunity, play for two to tie the score. You will have the psychological advantage during the extra end.

The Thirteenth End

An extra end requires a repetition of the strategy used when playing the twelfth end with the score tied. Physically, the advantage lies with the team having last rock, but, mentally, the other team, having come from behind to tie the game, have an edge. The more points they have scored to tie the game, the greater this advantage is. The psychological aspects of this, and its effect on team play, is reserved for the next chapter.

On looking back over the contents of this chapter on "Strategy in Skipping", I see that I may have exposed myself to the criticism that little consideration is given to the play of an average team of curlers, and also that reference was seldom made to peculiarities in ice conditions that alter strategical demands. I plead guilty on both counts for the reason that time and space do not permit a more elaborate examination of these problems.

As far as the average curler is concerned, I am sure that he realizes that even an expert team could not, by any stretch of the imagination, live up to the theoretically blueprinted requirements of a well-played end. All players have their weaknesses, and the skip in planning strategy must consider these first. I have played in bonspiels with green or inexperienced curlers where strategy was born out of desperation and was as unorthodox as the jump of a rabbit, yet there were many basic principles that I was able to employ effectively even in that type of competition.

What should be done and what can be done by a player are two different things, but an astute skip will certainly improve his skipping ability through experience and by the study of the methods of others. It is to this end that I have written this chapter.

Ice conditions affect strategy considerably. For example, wet or swingy ice makes accurate hitting very difficult so that the draw type of game is reverted to. Frosty ice and alkali ice similarly present the problem of using the draw game effectively, then the hitting style becomes more practical. Tricky ice with its "runs", "fall-backs", and ridges offers another challenge to the skip. Every sheet of ice has some trait or peculiarity that distinguishes it from the others. All this makes curling the fascinating, unpredictable game that it is. Whatever oddities of ice surface the skipper finds in his travels, the more experience he has had, and the more he understands the basic principles of directing the play of his team, the more he will enjoy meeting the challenge that is offered in each match he plays.

CHAPTER 5

The Psychology of Team Play

If perfection in curling could be achieved through the development of a well-co-ordinated delivery, sweeping ability, and a thorough
knowledge of skipping strategy, the game would lose its appeal for
thousands of devoted adherents. The real lure of the "roaring game"
lies in the element of surprise; the sudden changing of the tide when
an unbelievable rally turns defeat into victory; or the thrilling
accomplishment of upsetting a strong rink. It is truly said: "Curling
is a slippery game." That is why the word "IF" is displayed on
prominently placed signs in many curling clubs as a gentle reminder
to its members that the unexpected can and often will happen.

Because a curler is a human being and subject to a great variety
of emotions, impulses, and nerve reflexes, his state of mind
manoeuvres him into doing strange and unaccountable things during
a curling match. The outcome of a single stone will transform a
cool, confident player into a confused, erratic shotmaker. I have
witnessed an experienced skip, who had all the confidence in the
world, miss an easy shot early in the game, then become so unnerved
that he failed to make a single stone good thereafter. In another case,
a twelfth-end miss in an important bonspiel match upset a seasoned
skip so much that he never did regain his confidence.

The value and importance of understanding the use of psychology
in team play is greatly underestimated by curlers. Yet to my mind it
can be the greatest offensive weapon of a team. Any foursome that
has team spirit and morale, or whose members have developed and
maintained self-confidence in each other, is a difficult team to beat.
The skip who can create it is to be envied, but much of its potential
development depends on the other members of the rink, for their
co-operation, tolerance, and mutual respect is the foundation on
which team morale can be built. It would appear evident, then, that
this should be taken into consideration when selecting a team.

156

SELECTING A TEAM

Whenever old-time curlers start reminiscing about the good old days, they invariably drift into a discussion of the great teams of the past and present. The merits and demerits of each are debated for hours, and no matter how voluble the support, or how fluent the denial, when a team is mentioned, the final outcome is never of unanimous accord. But through all such endless dissertations, one common note can be detected. All the famous "powerhouse" rinks contained men who played their positions well and who co-ordinated with each other in shotmaking like a well-oiled machine. The deadly, almost monotonous consistency of their play, brought respect, and even fear, to the minds of their opponents, because they possessed, individually and collectively, not only the qualities mentioned in Chapter 3, but special skills demanded of them in the positions they played on the team.

The Lead

Should I be called upon to choose between a strong lead and a strong second, I would unhesitatingly select the strong lead every time. Without a doubt, he is the key-man of the "front end" of any team. His stones are, or should be, the first offensive threats of each end. The entire strategy of the end is built around the results of his shots, and as these are primarily draws, he should be a qualified expert at this sort of play. Similarly, it is every bit as important that he be accurate in "hitting the broom", so that his stone will come to rest on the exact spot you planned. If I had the space and the time, I could recount hundreds of cases where the first rock of an end was responsible for scoring a big end or winning a game. One incident will suffice. We were two-down coming home, in a Brier game against Johnny Franklin of Rosetown, Saskatchewan, and with last rock in our favour, Franklin decided to play the end wide open, so he signalled his lead to throw his first stone through the house. His men had been rifling fast shots at our draws all through the game with deadly accuracy so Johnny felt quite confident of the same strategy for the twelfth end. On the one side of the ice there was a definite ridge which extended from just beyond the hog-line to the back of the house. If our lead, Jimmy Grant, could place his draw up on top of that ridge, it would be a difficult stone to hit even with a fast-moving runner. I called Jim aside before the end commenced and said: "Jimmy, if you never get the broom in your life again, I'll forgive you, but this one we've got to have." His cheerful: "Good as done, Skipper", followed by a grin, belied his determination. His subsequent draw was perfect. It could not have been placed any better if he had carried it there. Although the Saskatchewan boys opened up their heavy artillery on this one piece of granite, their stones simply fanned the dust off as they whizzed by on either side. The spot where Jimmy's rock rested was accessible only by a slow draw which would climb far enough up the side of the ride to be out of range. While Franklin's men were firing at this stone, we drew three rocks to the other side of the rings but far enough back to tempt a double take-out off Jimmy's first effort. The, so called, "lowly" lead-man won that game and no one can ever take the credit away from him.

Too many curlers feel that if they can play draw shots well, no more should be expected of them, but the story above illustrates the necessity of being accurate in "getting the broom". This not only applies to draws, but to every type of shot he may be called on to make. By being accurate in placing his stones, he automatically gives his team the psychological edge. He helps to build up the confidence of the second man by making his co-players' shots as easy as possible, and at the same time his skip is able to take the fullest advantage of carrying out the strategy he has planned.

If any of you who are skips look back over games that you have won easily, you will find in most cases that your lead man was playing well. He was likely living up to the following requirements of a good lead:

1. Is good at draw-weight
2. Is accurate "on" the broom
3. Draws are of proper length
4. Has accurate length in placing stones in front of the rings
5. Has ability to draw behind guards
6. Is attentive to sweeping responsibilities

7. Is enthusiastic and interested in all shots
8. Compliments team mates on their play
9. Wastes no time getting into the hack
10. Shows willingness to practise after the game

A few of the famous leads I have played against who had all these qualities were Rae Stewart, Bill Grant of Winnipeg, and Hugh Miller, of Trail, B.C.

The Second

By the time the second man is ready to play, there may be three or four stones on or in front of the rings. Demands on his accuracy are even greater. His strength should lie in his ability to hit and roll, although, if the lead is playing well, the second may have as many or more draws as take-outs. A good second will be very proficient at quiet weight so that when he is asked to hit an opposing stone he can do so with just enough weight to go to the hack. Too many second players favour heavy weight for such shots because they feel more confident using such weight. This is a bad habit, and a second should curb his impulses and practise playing quiet weight until he is good at it. Fast stones played at this stage of the end seldom remain in the rings. They are certainly of little use behind the house.

The farther away a player gets from draw weight, the less chance for accuracy and consistency. Draw weight is the basis from which both player and skip should measure the weight required for any shot except a runner. A grade-A second is capable of playing the following weights:

1. Long guard weight
2. Medium length guard weight
3. Front ring weight
4. Tee-line weight or draw weight
5. Back ring weight
6. Light-hack weight
7. Hack weight
8. Heavy-hack weight
9. Runner weight

There is approximately six feet of difference in weight between each of these weight requirements, and any player who can play them all is a rare individual. Some curlers understand the first five, but when it comes to the last four, which apply to take-out shots, they are in a fog. Yet positional play of stones in building up an end depends almost entirely on accurate understanding and use of these weights.

The best second men I have known were quiet weight hitters and therefore very reliable at draw weight. Marvin Macintyre, who played with me at second rock for over ten years, was a specialist at nudging opposition rocks from the rings, and, as a result, he could draw to a dime any time it was required. Cliff Hudson, Ron Singbush, Vic Wood, Marno Frederickson, Bill McKnight and Lyle Dyker were others I have known who excelled at this position, and all of them played on Canadian Championship rinks.

The Third or Vice-Skip

The third player must be a shot-maker par excellence, a strategist, and a good judge of ice and weight. He is the clean-up man of the rink as it is often his responsibility to open up the end to make it possible for the skip to get a clear shot at the rings or to break up a bad combination of opposing rocks in the house. When the skip's strategy backfires, or the lead and second stones are ineffective, the third man is called upon to remedy the situation. His shots are frequently multiple-duty ones, where one of his well-directed stones will scatter two or three guards or effect a double raise, strike and roll behind a guard, make a double wick, draw a port, or clean out a cluster of enemy rocks. Essentially, he must have hairpin accuracy in swinging at the broom, and be astute in estimating the weight required so that he can play confidently for rolls, ports, and wicks. The harder the shot, the more his concentrative ability and the greater his confidence. This may sound like a skip speaking who expects his third to be a miracle man so that he (the skip) will not have to make any difficult shots himself. But I can assure you that when a team is playing percentages and winning consistently, the skip will have to do his share of the play-making, too; but as his stones are the last two of the end, he must be in a position to make them count if the team expects to keep its win and loss ratio in proper balance.

As the third man is the vice-skip, he should know the "run" of the ice almost as well as the skip. Only when he does will he have sufficient confidence to make the shots required of him. When the skip plays his stones, the third takes over the reins as the director of sweeping so he must be a good judge of weight in appraising a stone approaching the rings. A good third man never leaves his position on the "head" while directing the sweepers. He will remain in a position from which he can best watch both the direction and the weight of an incoming rock. He will be alert to rolls, wicks, and raises, and quick to sweep any moving stones in the rings (that the rule allows) to better their strategic position. There is no denying that a vice-skip on the tee-line, who is an alert opportunist, can do much toward bolstering the mental attitude of all members of the team. It takes only one moment of careless indifference on his part, say in neglecting to sweep an opponent's rock out of the rings, to undermine the morale of his team mates. They will feel that he did not do all he could to help the cause, and their feelings, although not expressed verbally, will register in a noticeable slackening of enthusiasm. Many individual curlers have not the common sense to realize that their individual attitudes affect the play of the rest of the team. They are smugly complacent about how important their own shots are, but fail to understand that the other fellow feels the same way. Only when they learn to put as much energy and enthusiasm into other shots as they do into their own will they become ideal members of a rink.

One over-worked theory—that the skip's authority is absolute and final in the selection of the shot to be played—is utterly foolish in its concept as far as the third man is concerned. Under no circumstances should any player be asked to make a shot that he has absolutely no confidence in, and this applies particularly in the case of the vice-skip. Any suggestion that the skip of a curling team is entitled to exercise "Divine Right" in directing play is foreign to the democratic tendencies of the game. Naturally, the team requires a skipper, but not one of a Captain Bligh disposition. If there is a difference of opinion concerning a choice of shots, it should be discussed by the skip and third, and if the shot involves strategy only but not the difficulty of making it, then agreement should be arrived at. If this cannot be achieved, the vice-skip should play the shot he deems advisable because he has complete confidence that it is the correct one and he will more than likely make it. Otherwise, if he is asked to play his stone according to the skip's idea, he will do so with grave doubt and uncertainty in his mind. Should he miss the shot, he will inwardly blame the skip for his failure and his mental attitude will suffer considerably. However, if the shot in question is a matter of confidence in the ability to make it, the skip has no alternative but to have his vice-skip play the one he feels certain he can make. More potentially good teams render themselves ineffective through this breach of confidence between the skip and his third man than through any other cause. The same attitude should prevail when the skip's shot is planned. There is not much use being stubborn and proud about it. Get rid of your individual likes and dislikes as far as the other man is concerned. Curling is a team game, so subordinate your pride to the better interests of team play. Talk over the shot if you must, but let the man who is to play the shot make the final decision. He will maintain his confidence, and, having made the final decision, he will assume the responsibility, and, knowing this, he will usually make the shot. Even if the strategy is wrong, he will rarely execute a shot that he is not confident of making.

I may be prejudiced in believing that my brother Grant is the best third man of all time. He is as good a skipping strategist as I, or better than I. His brilliant shot-making ability at third rock has made me look good on numerous occasions, and his keen analysis of ice has saved the day in many a close-scoring game. As a clean-up man he has few equals, for he has the confidence and the hitting ability to play for the corners and the narrow ports if the occasion demands. The harder the shot, the better he likes it, and the more he concentrates in his determination to make it. Strange to relate, he plays more brilliantly if I am off colour, whereas if he has a bad game, the calibre of my play increases correspondingly. Through mutual confidence and understanding, he selects his own shot unless another is mentioned that he has overlooked, and vice versa when my turn comes. As a result, each of us builds up his own morale and self-confidence, and, indirectly, that of lead and second with it. "Bung" Cartmell, of Glenboro, was Ab Gowanlock's famous clean-up man, one of the deadliest sharp-shooters of them all. Jimmy Congalton, Alex Welsh, Lorne Stewart, Ernie Pollard, Frank Cassidy, Sam Penwarden, and many others too numerous to mention, possessed the fundamental qualities that made them all outstanding as vice-skips.

The Skip

There are many varieties of the species referred to as skips. One may be revered as a brilliant strategist if he has a team strong enough to win a championship, but if he has an average team who expect him to draw to the "button" end after end to save the day, he is just another name on the entry list. If his rink think that he is a good skipper, his rock is placed at the hack for him when it is his turn to play, his coffee is ready and waiting at the conclusion of the game, and he may even get a drive home in the lead's new automobile. But if he doesn't rate in that category, he retrieves his own stones at the hack, buys coffee for the rink, drives them home, and recounts the latest stories to keep them in good humour.

Be it as it may, the skip has his problems on and off the ice. His chief responsibility on the ice is to direct the play in addition to making his own shots count. Most curlers are human and good fellows, but they expect certain qualities in a good skip.

Qualifications of a Skip

In addition to being a good shot-maker and having all the qualities he demands of his players (see Chapter 3), a good skip should possess these additional abilities:

Ability to: 1. Judge ice for his players
2. Size up weaknesses of opponents
3. Determine style of play or strategy required
4. Control his emotions
5. Build up team morale and confidence
6. Out-guess or out-manoeuvre the opposing skip
7. Select a well-balanced rink
8. Be daring when the occasion demands

The list of qualities demanded of a skip sets a very high standard, and it would require a combination of saint and field general to produce such a person, nevertheless all skips are guilty of the omission of one or more of the qualities their team mates would like them to possess, so if you are a skip you might just as well examine yourself in the mirror of other curlers' eyes and try to remedy your deficiencies as you see them. If you desire to build the efficiency of your team play to its greatest potential, you must first acquaint yourself with the simple rules that govern human motivation. It is quite possible to take an average curler, and by encouragement and inspiration, build up his confidence in himself and you to a point where he will make an amazing number of good shots. The story appears in reverse when a good curler can become, through discouragement, criticism, or indifference from his skip, a very erratic player.

Building up Team Morale and Self-Confidence

Sometimes it is easier to list faults than virtues, because there is a tendency to look for them instead of trying to seek out the good points. But there are many indifferent idiosyncracies prevailing among skips who err in handling their players that I will venture to offer a few suggestions in the hope that they will be of value to skips who haven't formed too many bad habits.

1. If one of your players misses a shot, do not show your annoyance or disgust by word, gesture, or facial expression. He will feel badly enough about it without your adding to his discomfort. He will also resent it, and will be consciously thinking of it when he plays his next stone. Be cheerful and call down to him: "All right, John. You'll get it next time!" or wave at him and grin. If you get a chance when he comes up the ice, speak to him quietly and talk over the shot with him. If it is necessary to maintain his confidence, accept the blame for his miss, but under no circumstances, blame him.

2. When a player makes a good shot, tell him so. Don't keep it a secret. Be enthusiastic and pleased about it. Make him feel he is right on his game and he will continue to make his shots. If he gets the broom perfectly, or the weight, but not the perfect shot you wanted, assure him that the ice or weight he used was right. He will feel much better after that.

3. If you happen to have discussed a strategic shot with your vice-skip and have come to a decision, don't be afraid to explain it to your sweepers as you walk down the ice to make the shot. They like to think they are in the game, too, and they will take more interest in the shot. If it be a particularly crucial decision, call them into the huddle with your third man and make the decision together. Then if the shot is missed or does not work out as hoped, they will feel part of the responsibility and will not shift the entire blame to you and your third. Consequently, there will be no "mutterings under the beard".

4. Encourage your men to keep up their will to win, even when the score is against you. Be an optimist. Optimism is contagious.

5. Praise your sweepers after they have worked hard to get a stone into position. Give them the credit for doing it, if it is your rock. Don't strut back to the tee as if you were solely responsible.

6. Help your sweepers when you get a chance. Let them know you are co-operating.

7. Show self-confidence at all times, but not conceit. If your players get the feeling that you are fairly sure of yourself, they will gain more confidence in your judgment when you estimate the ice and weight required for their shots. Do not carry the confidence so far that you exhibit lack of confidence in the judgment of your team mates. This will cause them to lean on you and thus to lose confidence in themselves. Ask them now and again what turn or amount of ice they prefer. Keep up their self-reliance whatever happens. Do not be too decisive or too positive. It sometimes causes indecision and uncertainty in the minds of your men. Keep them in the game with you and make it necessary for them to share the responsibility in judging ice and weight. All is lost if they ever reach the point where they rely solely on your judgment. Keep them thinking and concentrating on the game.

8. Be alert on the "head" to capitalize on rubs, rolls, or wicks by your own men or the opposition. Never give your players the impression that you are not on the job.

9. If you miss one of your own shots, don't blame the sweepers

or the third man. Be a man. Swallow your disappointment and say, "Sorry, boys. I'll get it next time."

10. Know your men. Play to their strong points. Don't ask them for a difficult shot early in the game. Consider the possibilities of making a shot and pass it up if the odds are against it, even though it disturbs your strategy. One miss by a player early in the game undermines his confidence.

A Well-Balanced Team

Four skips seldom make a good combination as a rink because they usually favour different styles of play, and are often satisfied that the other members of the team are inferior in ability, either as shotmakers or as strategists. They are inclined to be critical of each other, and as each has had experience reading ice and directing play, they mentally question the judgment of whoever has the responsibility of being skip. As long as they are winning, any lack of harmony is not evident, but as soon as the decision goes against them, the smouldering embers of dissatisfaction break into open flames.

It is feasible for four skips to play on the same team if all are unreservedly satisfied with the choice of skip, his style of play, have complete confidence in each other, and have sufficient interest in common to synchronize their personalities in the interests of harmonized team play. Even then a "packed" rink has a disadvantage, for the perspective of the play from the side ice is altogether different from the picture a skip gets on the tee-line. It takes years of practice to judge ice from the side of the sheet.

If I had the opportunity to select a team from an unlimited number of curlers, I might go so far as to choose a skip as a third man, but I would forget the seasoned skips from there on. In casting about for a lead and second, I would look for men who had years of experience playing in those positions.

During the past four years, Charlie Read has filled capably the position of lead on our rink. Previous to joining the team he had played in that position for at least three years, so he is well adjusted to the requirements of a good lead. In addition, he possesses the personal qualities so necessary to team morale, and therefore has been a valuable cog in our curling machine. Lyle Dyker has had more than twelve years experience playing second stone, seven of them with us. Lyle has had his bad days and his good days, but has an exceptionally fine mental attitude that contributes to the self-confidence of the other members of the rink. I can say without fear of contradiction that during the past few years that Charlie, Lyle, Grant and I have been curling together, there has been nothing but mutual respect, admiration, and complete co-operation and harmony during each and all of our games. During the Canadian Championships at Hamilton in 1949, particularly, team morale with the four of us reached a very high standard. We kept up a continual chatter of encouragement, praise, and congratulatory comments to each other, with the effect that in my thirty-odd years of curling, I have never played on a team whose play was so inspired. I put it all down to the wonderful team spirit that existed among us.

Psychology in Strategy and Play

A skip is wise to remember that the mental attitude of the members of an opposing rink will seriously affect their efficiency as shot makers, and the confidence exhibited by a rival skip has a great bearing on the soundness of his tactical play. Any shot, or the play of any end, that disrupts this equilibrium will have disastrous effects on team morale. When you score a big end on an average team, their mental depression is quite noticeable. Many rinks play according to the score board. If they are even, or a few points up, they play as if inspired, but if they are on the short end of the score, their play is listless and half-hearted. It was for this reason that I switched my type of strategy several years ago. Now, instead of having the lead place his first stone in front of the rings when the opposition has last rock, he draws to the side of the house. Our logic is that our team is expert enough at both hitting and drawing to play the end wide open. If the opposing skip makes his last stone, well enough. He is entitled to count one. But if he is faced with three or four of our stones in the house when he plays this rock, the thoughts that are going through his mind before he delivers will cause him far more mental anguish than if he were called upon to draw around a guard to cut us out of one shot. Even though we have three or four unguarded stones in the rings when he plays, because his shot is relatively simple, he will

worry more about missing it and letting us score three or four than
he will if he is confronted with a more difficult situation. Five times
out of ten he will not make the shot, and thereafter he will lose his
confidence, and so will his team. We have played scores of games
where the opposing skip has made his shot in such situations for
many ends, but sooner or later he has missed one. Nothing is more
disheartening to a rink than the score of a big end against them, and
particularly when the skip has last rock. The simpler the shot missed,
the greater the loss of team morale.

Do not over-estimate the ability of your opposition. They are
human like yourself and miss a shot once in a while, no matter how
great their reputation. Put your rocks in the rings and put it up to
them to get them out. If there are four or five stones against you,
don't get panicky and start blasting. Draw one into the rings if it is
your last stone and give your opposing skip the responsibility of
removing it if he wants to score a big end. Should he miss, he will
never regain his confidence. But if you blast at his stone with your
last rock and roll out, there is no pressure left on him at all; all he
has to do is draw to the rings. This will be easy because he has
nothing to lose. I am sure Jack Caldwell of Hamiota, Man., will
forgive me for recalling a game in the Winnipeg Bonspiel where he
was four points up on us playing the eighth. To make matters worse,
he was lying four or five when I came to play my last stone and he
also had the advantage of last rock. I finally decided to draw. My
stone stopped on the four-foot ring and was wide open. All Jack had
to do was pass it through for a six and we could leave for home. How
he missed I'll never know, because Jack is a fine curler, but miss he
did and we went on to win the game. His costly error completely
demoralized his men, and he himself hardly made a shot thereafter.
On the other hand, our team, given a new lease on life, after very
spotty playing during the first eight ends, began to curl well again.

During the early stages of the game, try to set up your stones to
encourage a few misses by your opponents. Two or three misses will
gradually give them the idea that they are "off their game" that day,
and their curling will suffer accordingly. Some years ago, we were
drawn against a smart young team in bonspiel play. One of the

players had a bit of conceit in him, although an excellent curler. When playing well, he was very sure of himself, so we decided that we would try to confront him with a difficult shot or two early in the game. As luck would have it he missed his two shots in the third end, both of which were tricky to make. He curled erratically until the tenth end but by that time we had assumed a moderate but strategical lead in score. Conversely, when asking for shots from your own rink during the early ends, see to it that you select shots that they can make easily to help bolster confidence. If a shot stone is partially hidden by a guard, for example, don't ask for a difficult draw around the guard to push the shot back, rather call for a two-way shot, either to squeeze past the guard and chip out the shot stone, or to remove the guard. If he makes either, he will feel he has done his duty.

Psychology in Strategy During the Last Ends

The intense nervous tension and mental pressure existing in a close-scoring game during the last three ends requires the maintenance of a high degree of morale in a team. Every stone played and every strategical decision made by the skip will swing the pendulum one way or the other. The most common error committed by skips at this point is to change the style of play. This is a desperate measure employed by a skip who is many points in arrears, but for the pilot of a rink who is leading at this stage to change from the offensive to defensive is asking for trouble in large doses. Too many games are thrown away when a skip suddenly decides to protect his lead instead of adding to it. For no apparent reason he asks his men to fire at everything in sight. A few misses occur. Fear creeps in, followed by panic. Draw weight is lost, and he and his men reel under the impact of a big end scored against them, and the opposition is back in the game again. Now the psychological advantage is held by the other team and unless they commit the same blunder in the next end, the damage is done.

From the tenth end on, it is necessary to maintain any score advantage you may have, and this can be done only by keeping the offensive pressure on the opposition. Even the loss of two points, if you are five up, causes your men to cast furtive glances at the scoreboard. Keep your team using the same hitting weight as before, so that they are delivering their stones in a normal, unhurried, and rhythmic motion. It will help them to relax and concentrate on swinging at the broom. The chief reason for so many misses by a player is that he, sensing the urgency of removing an opponent's rock at this crucial point, thinks too much of the stone he is asked to hit, and it looms so large in his mind that he forgets about the broom during his swing and aims at the rock. This is even more apparent when the skip calls for an over-weight shot where very little ice is needed. Every player should make up his mind while in the hack to do two things:

1. Decide what weight he is going to play
2. Convince himself that he must forget the rock he is trying to hit and concentrate on swinging at the broom.

Another point worth mentioning here concerns a well known fact that most take-outs are missed by being narrow of the broom rather than by being wide. The explanation of this lies in the mental attitude of the player ready to deliver his stone. In his anxiety to hit the rock, it becomes more important in his mind than the position of the skip's broom, and although he looks at the broom during part of his swing, his eyes at the last moment, unconsciously move to the rock he is to hit, and subconsciously this affects his swing. Just remember that if your stone is ten inches wide and the rock you are to hit is the same, you have a striking area of twenty inches to utilize. If you swing at the rock instead of the broom you are cutting this area to ten inches, or exactly one-half.

Only in playing the twelfth or thirteenth ends is a change in the style of play excusable, and then only when you are trying to keep the front open for last rock, or you want to prevent the possibility of your opponents using your stones for backing. Otherwise do not risk upsetting the advantage your team may have. The team coming from behind has the more aggressive mental attitude, and the greater the gap they have closed, the more their confidence. There is only one way to curb this upsurge of optimism, and that is to get back into the driver's seat again by taking the offensive and playing quietel weight. Call "time out" if you like and get into a huddle with your players. Crack a joke and relieve the tension. I remember in one of these huddles during a very disastrous-looking twelfth end, our lead brought a laugh by saying: "I'll go into the clubhouse and phone mother to ask what she would do." We all felt better after that and settled down.

Studying Your Opponents' Weaknesses

After many seasons of play you will be familiar with your club-mates' weaknesses and they with yours, but when it comes to bonspiel play against unfamiliar rinks, you will have to start from scratch, and if you are watchful, the game will not have progressed very far before you will have spotted a flaw or two in the deliveries of opposing players, or in the strategy of the rival skip. In competitive play, it is important to take advantage of these faults to keep the offensive edge.

(a) WEAKNESSES OF PLAYERS

1. Inaccuracy at hitting with either turn. Many curlers are very weak at hitting with an out-turn. Play your stones so that such a player will be forced to play as many out-turns as possible.

2. Wide with either turn. Play your stones on runs in the ice where accuracy on the broom is essential for hitting.

3. Poor "hitters". Place your stones in front of the tee so that a draw is impossible. If the entire team is poor at hitting, play the ends wide open. Do not give them any protection for their draws.

4. Good hitters but poor at the draw. Protect your draws and force them to draw. Score in the early ends to get the advantage. Do not allow such a rink to get the jump on you or they will be hard to catch.

5. Excitable, erratic players. Play for a miss if it will give you a chance to build an end.

(b) WEAKNESSES OF OPPOSING SKIP

1. Dislikes to draw. Play short guards and tempt him to hit them.

2. Dislikes hitting. Play your stones in the four-foot circle in front of the tee-line.

3. Fears guards or rocks in front of the house. Place more stones in front of the rings, and raise them in later.

One skip I knew worried considerably over a stone in front of the house when he had last rock. His anxiety revealed itself in his gestures and instructions to his men. Next end I had our lead play both his stones in front, even though the other lead drew his first stone to the side rings. When I took a look at the other skip to see how this strategy registered, I could hardly believe what I saw. He was literally purple. I am hesitant to admit that it became a practice to place two stones in front whenever I played that skip thereafter.

4. Likes playing for double take-outs. Spread the stones at a tempting angle. Let him throw to his heart's content. He will not make very many of them and his stone will usually roll out of the rings if he does hit one of yours.

5. Guards shot rock even though he has last stone. Have your players play back-ring weight, just enough to rub the guard off and roll into the rings. If he keeps doing this long enough, you'll have a house full, and with one missed guard he will be confronted with a good-sized nightmare.

6. Ignores your stones just in front of the rings. Raise them in or split them in with the "shooter", when the opportunity arises.

7. Fails to watch the ice. Try an experimental draw to an unexplored side of the sheet if you get a chance.

Mental Hazards

A good many curlers are mentally agitated or irritated to the point of distraction by the simplest of things. Yet anything that disturbs an individual's confidence or interrupts his concentration while making a shot is serious. When nervous tension is geared up, and competitive temperaments are at a fever pitch, minor disturbances create no end of irritation and even cause bitter feelings.

There are four classes of mental hazards:

      1. Other players
      2. Playing conditions
      3. Noises
      4. Superstitions

1. OTHER PLAYERS

Some of the actions of other players are inexcusable, particularly when they are knowingly perpetrated for the sole purpose of distracting the opponent. Curling as a rule is played by a grand bunch of fellows, but there are a few "untouchables" in every club who spoil the good sportsmanship the game is noted for. Fortunately these individuals do not wear too well with their fellow curlers, and they eventually leave the club. Here are a few intolerable hazards of this category.

(a) Moving back and forth behind the skip's broom at the other end of the ice when a player is set to deliver his stone. The only way to handle this is to stop your delivery and ask the offender to stand still.

(b) A player standing too close to the hack when you are set for delivery. Mostly such position is unintentional.

(c) Moving across the ice as you deliver.

(d) Talking loudly within ear shot when you are in the hack.

(e) Uncalled-for remarks by opposing players before you go down the ice to make your shot. How an individual can stoop to this practice I do not know. It is a subversive attempt to upset you. I have had this happen several times but have simply ignored it. It usually backfires on them because my concentration in making the shot is all the more intense as a result.

(f) Name rinks. To many teams, playing against a famous rink is a definite hazard. On one occasion Leo Johnson of Winnipeg was playing a young rink from rural Manitoba in the Winnipeg Bonspiel, and at the eighth end the game was tied. At that moment the young skip, who had been playing a wonderful game, happened to look at a crest on Leo Johnson's sweater. When he saw the words "Canadian Champions" inscribed thereon he went into a sudden tailspin and he and his team "blew up" completely. We have won a lot of games on our reputation more than on our curling, only because we try to score during the first few ends so that if the opposition has this in mind it will tend to stay there. But there is no plausible excuse for a team to get "buck fever" when playing a name rink. It would be better if they made the renowned foursome beat them on the ice rather than in the hotel room.

2. Playing Conditions

Wet ice, frosty ice, bad hacks, tricky or crooked ice, chipped ice in front of the hack, all provide mental hazards, and with some curlers it becomes such an obsession that it completely ruins their effectiveness. A final game in the Kenora, Ontario, bonspiel was played on a sheet of ice that was badly cut up at the hack. Three of us on our team just ignored it and concentrated on swinging at the broom, happen what may. The fourth member let it bother him so much he rarely made a shot. The opposing rink all went to pieces. They seemed to be glad to use it as an excuse. There is power in mind over matter. If you make up your mind and forget everything else, it is surprising how well you can do under such conditions. It is exactly the same for the opposition so no one team has the advantage. Do not get into the habit of making excuses for missing shots. You are simply trying to cover an inferiority complex which should not exist in the first place.

3. Noises

Loud reports of a rock crashing into the back-boards, or striking other rocks; the sudden roar of a crowd; the bellowing of another skip; the talking of spectators or the roar of a passing street car, are problems affecting all players. The best practice is to wait until the noise subsides then settle yourself in the hack to make your shot. Both Grant and I wear hearing aids and have been jokingly accused of having an advantage because we can shut them off. We have tried it, but it does not work for we do not feel natural, nor would anyone else if the normal sounds were shut out.

4. Superstitions

Curlers succumb to the apparent influence of outside factors on their wins and losses just as players in other sports do. For several years we associated Number 13 with our failures as it seemed that we could win twelve games in a row but always faltered when it came to the thirteenth. Having press photos taken before a final match was a pet aversion of one of our men and he constantly balked every time this was proposed. He became even more adamant after we persuaded him on one occasion then lost the match afterwards.

It is simply an association of ideas but I have always respected the superstitions of any of my players, because I want them to preserve the happiest state of mind possible. I have had my own superstitious associations, too. One of the most ridiculous, but one which I rigidly adhered to for fear of breaking the spell, was the route to the curling club. There were ten ways of getting there but I followed the "charmed" path every time, even to the point of coming back and starting out again if I absent-mindedly took the wrong turn.

Offensive and Defensive Play

It is about time I cleaned up the thoughts I have in mind when referring to offensive and defensive strategy, which terms I have used several times in previous pages. My theory, termed by some as unusual, is that a skip is using offensive play when he asks for a draw, and is acting defensively when he signals a take-out. Even in the case where an opponent lies six or seven shots, to play a draw is an offensive action. But as soon as a skip starts to direct his players to remove opposition rocks he is commencing defensive action. It is the use of defensive play that leads to the creation of havoc in the mind of a player because it requires unerring accuracy to hit well enough to keep rocks in play. During the later stages of a game it is the sudden switch from a draw, or offensive game, to hitting, or defensive play, that causes so much grief. Some defensive play is necessary, but if the members of a team are accurate with their draws, little defensive action will be needed. By consistent draws, the opposing team is kept on the defensive continually, and if their stones do remain in the rings, only a quiet removal is necessary. The heavier the weight played in hitting, the greater the defensive action, and the greater the importance the skip attaches to the necessity for it. In reality he is retreating with the spoils, and fighting a rearguard action. When a skip is a few points up and resorts to defensive strategy entirely, he is employing the "hit and run" tactics. When he allows the other team to take the offensive away from him, he is exposing his rink to its greatest vulnerability. Only on the last end should he resort to it.

Earlier in the game, the use of heavy defensive play usually indicates lack of confidence or a wavering uncertainty on the part of the skip. Of course it is necessary to remove opposing rocks, but by using just over back-ring weight a skip is calling for a mild type of defensive play. The chief object of the game is to score yourself, not just to try to keep the other fellow from scoring. The only way to score that I know of is to place your stones in the rings. Guards are defensive in nature and must be used occasionally to protect an offensive position, but essentially an offensive draw game will place the greatest pressure on the opponents, and the continuation of this pressure during every end will get results.

Once again, in case the statements above are misconstrued, I refer only to ice with a keen surface where the draw game can be played most effectively. No aspersions are suggested, either, to such fine-hitting rinks as Jimmy Welsh's of Winnipeg, who use the running game. The Welsh rink is expert at the offensive draw game, too, but the strategy they use against a good draw team is to cut down the score if their opponents threaten.

As it is time for me to conclude these pages, I want to express the hope that you will have gained something of value to add to your increasing enjoyment of a great competitive, yet sociable, game. As for myself, I have derived much pleasure in compiling this edition and recapturing many of the thrills and memories of former experiences on the ice, although, once this book is published, I dare not miss a shot or commit a strategical error!

Although this book is written primarily for the competitive curler who desires to improve his game, I cannot conclude without reference to the thousands of players who play the game for sociability's sake and because they love it.

Of the estimated 200,000 curlers in the world, there is not one who would not derive a real thrill out of being a member of a Championship team whether it meant the winning of a District Bonspiel, an Automobile Bonspiel, or the Macdonald Brier Tankard. We all love the thrill of achievement. Yet there are many to whom it happens seldom, and many more who never have reached the winner's circle. In order to have winners we must have losers, and the losers naturally form the great bulk of the membership of our grand fraternity. If it were not for their increasing interest in the game, and their unselfish devotion to building up the wonderful spirit of sportsmanship that exists among curlers, there would be no such game for the winners. Many of the better curlers overlook this simple truth and forget to put back into the pastime something in repayment for the satisfaction and pleasure it has given them.

A great number of hard-working organizers and executives of thousands of curling clubs all over this and other continents have contributed unstintingly of their time and energy to do the work of financing, programming, and planning so that the game can go on— so that curlers can curl. These men, behind the scenes, when prizes are distributed and trophies presented, represent the backbone of curling. To them I doff my hat!

3 4 5 6 7 8 9   75 74 73 72